THE CONCEPT OF HUMAN RIGHTS

The Concept of Human Rights

Jack Donnelly

College of the Holy Cross
Worcester, Massachusetts

ST. MARTIN'S PRESS
New York

Library of Congress Cataloging in Publication Data

Donnelly, Jack
    The concept of human rights.

    Revision of thesis (Ph. D.)—University of
California, Berkeley, 1981.
    Bibliography: p.
    Includes index.
    1. Civil rights.   I. Title.
JC571.D74   1985   323.4   84-22863
ISBN 0-312-15941-2

CONTENTS

The rank is but the guinea stamp,
The man's the gold, for all that.

Traditional

ACKNOWLEDGEMENTS

This is a revision of my doctoral dissertation, submitted at the University of California, Berkeley, in the autumn of 1981. Hanna Pitkin laboured through numerous drafts of the dissertation with uncommon care and unfailing good humour and support — so much so that I actually enjoyed the usually painful process of writing a dissertation. Ernie Haas also was most helpful as a second reader. I hope that in the distance between the dissertation and this book they will see some enduring results of their teaching, advice and support.

In the dissertation stage, Pat Boling, Don Downs, Steph Haggard and Gregg Kvistad read individual chapters or helped me think through important issues. Since then, Charlie Brockett has provided helpful comments on what is now Chapter 3. Preston King made several useful suggestions for narrowing and focusing my argument. Rhoda Howard read the entire manuscript and helped me to clarify and simplify the presentation of a number of important points.

Throughout it all, Cathy has always been there. This book is as much hers as mine.

1 INTRODUCTION: BEING RIGHT AND HAVING A RIGHT

Introduction and Overview

What are human rights? Literally, they are the rights of humans. More precisely, human rights are the rights one has simply because one is a human being. This book is devoted to exploring the dimensions and implications of this deceptively simple answer.

Three major levels or parts can be distinguished in the theory of human rights:

(1) the *nature* of human rights (What kind of a 'thing' is a human right and how does it 'work'?);
(2) their *source* (From what or where do we get human rights?); and
(3) their *substance* or *specification* (What are the particular things to which we have human rights? What is on the 'list' of human rights?).

While the third level certainly is the ultimate theoretical objective, I shall concentrate on the first two because of their logical priority as well as my inability to provide an adequate philosophical justification of a particular list, for reasons that should become clear after the discussion of the source of human rights in Chapter 3.

Everything that is on a list of human rights — any list — is a human right. Our concern will be with the meaning, source and implications of inclusion on such a list, with what it means, not only logically but behaviourally, to be able to say '*x* is a human right' or 'I have a human right to *x*'. What sort of obligations do human rights impose? How, and on whom? How are claims of human rights related to other claims that may be made on persons and institutions in a position to provide or deny *x*? What is their moral foundation? How would the world be different if they were not available?

The literal definition of human rights as the *rights* of *humans* provides the structure for the first half of the book. In this chapter, following this very brief overview, we will begin to clarify the meaning of 'rights' by distinguishing two important senses of the

1

term 'right'. The distinction between something *being* right and someone *having* a right provides the conceptual core around which the book revolves. Chapter 2 then explores some of the ways rights 'work', both in general and, in its final section, with special reference to *human* rights.

In Chapter 3 we turn to the source of human rights; roughly, to the meaning of 'human' in 'human rights'. I argue that socially shared moral conceptions of the nature of the human person and the conditions necessary for a life of dignity are the source of human rights. What distinguishes human rights from other moral ideals, however, is that they take the form of rights, a particular kind of institution and instrument.

Combining these accounts of the nature and source of human rights yields what I call the 'constructivist' theory of human rights: the underlying moral vision of human nature, if expressed and implemented in the form of human rights, will actually *create* the envisioned person, so long as it lies within the psycho-biological and social limits of human possibility. Thus human rights represent a special sort of self-fulfilling moral prophecy and provide a plan for the construction of a political regime in which a truly human being can lead a life of dignity, developing and expressing the moral possibilities of human nature.

While this account of the nature and source of human rights is essentially original, I prefer to stress its descriptive character. People do claim human rights, and have done so for at least two or three centuries. Such claims, I am painfully aware, have been subject to an incredible variety of abuses, both vicious and innocent. None the less, the still deep resonances of a document such as the French *Declaration of the Rights of Man and the Citizen*, the remarkably wide acceptance, in word and aspiration if not in deed, of more recent documents such as the *Universal Declaration of Human Rights*, and the persistent use of claims of human rights, despite theoretical dismissals and widespread political violations, suggest a core of meaning beyond abusive misappropriations of the rhetoric of human rights.

I believe that most of us have an intuitive grasp of this meaning and some of its most important political implications, in spite of our difficulty in making it explicit. My goal here is to explicate this understanding; this is what conceptual analysis, as I understand it, is about. The real test of the constructivist theory, then, is its ability to capture and elucidate our intuitive sense of 'human rights'. Therefore, the theory is 'descriptive': although about one of our most important and politically profound moral notions, it aims to describe the way 'human rights' function in our language and political practice, how people use 'human rights', and what they mean when they claim them.

Needless to say, human rights represent but one of many ways that have been or might be tried for organising political life. Although there is neither space nor reason to explore all the alternatives, a consideration of some of the more prominent ones — natural law, utilitarianism, prescription, Marxism, and syncretic Third World conceptions of 'human rights' — is offered in Chapters 4 and 5. The purpose of these comparisons is to elaborate the distinctive nature of the human rights approach to human dignity and political organisation, and provide a limited and partial argument for preferring the human rights approach. Finally, in a brief postscript, I touch on the problem of lists of human rights.

Being Right and Having a Right

For all their differences from other types of rights, human rights are *rights*. Therefore, the first order of business, which will occupy us through most of this and the following chapter, is to analyse the concept of rights. The starting point for this enterprise is the distinction between something *being* right and someone *having* a right to something.

The word 'right' encompasses at least two concepts of great political and moral significance. On the one hand, 'right' refers to *moral righteousness*, as in 'It's just not the right thing to do!' On the other hand, 'right' may refer to *entitlement*, as in the claim 'I have a right to . . .' This second sense of entitlement distinguishes *rights*, human or otherwise.

These two senses of 'right' have very different philosophical 'grammars,' indicative of important differences in these two concepts that share a single word. When we talk of righteousness, the verb generally used is 'to be' — for example, 'It is right for you to help him', 'What is it right to do here?' 'It wouldn't be right to leave now'. Therefore, I will refer to this sense as 'right in the sense of "what is right" ' and speak of something being right. When speaking of entitlements, however, 'to be' is rarely if ever used. Instead, we talk of 'having' or 'holding' rights, and of various ways of using the rights one 'has'. I will refer to this as 'right in the sense of "having a right" '.

To say that something *is* right points to conformity with a standard of righteousness; '*x* is right' is a judgement of *x*'s rectitude, as defined by established standards. As a result, right in the sense of 'what is right' is used primarily as an adjective or adverb. In contrast, right in the sense of 'having a right' is almost always used as a substantive, and only in this sense do we speak of 'a right' or 'rights' in the plural (except for relatively rare locutions such as 'the rights and wrongs of capital punishment'). Rights are 'things' that one 'has', 'holds' and may 'exercise' or otherwise put to use. One cannot possess, but only be in accord with, the (standard of) right, whereas having a right is crucial.

While 'right' in both senses expresses or imposes obligation, who is obliged, the type of obligation, and the relationships between the parties depend largely on the sense in question. Consider the paradigmatic claim 'It *is right* for A to do *x* (with respect to B)'. Here A is obliged by the righteousness of doing *x*, and the obligation associated with *x* *being* right is primarily an obligation to perform an act (because it is right). A's obligation is *to do x*; the rectitude of doing *x*, in itself, creates the obligation. That it is done in relation to B (rather than C or D) is largely incidental. Thus we characteristically speak of some*thing* being right.

But when A *has* a right to *x* with respect to B, B is obliged by the 'right', and his obligation is primarily to a person (to A). Here the intrinsic nature of *x* is a secondary consideration; B's obligation arises primarily from the fact that A *has a right* to *x*, and therefore is owed *x*. For example, contracts and promises may establish (prima facie) obligations by conferring rights to actions or holdings that have no intrinsic moral relevance. Thus we characteristically speak of some*one* having a right.

These contrasting emphases on the action and on the person arise primarily from the entitlement provided by rights. Being right establishes duties, but nothing more. However, to have a right to *x* is to be *entitled* to *x*, to be owed *x*. Therefore, to fail to respect someone's rights is not just bad or wrong and a failure to discharge a duty; it is a special and particularly serious affront to that person.

Titles serve as proof or justification. Having a right/title to *x* provides (prima facie) justification for having, doing or enjoying *x*, independent of considerations of what is good or right. We can see this in claims such as 'It's mine; I'm entitled to it' or 'You're entitled to do it whether he likes it or not'.

To capture this prima facie priority of rights over other justifying principles, Dworkin (1977: xi, 90) speaks of rights as 'trumps'. Rights are not just one type of moral or social goal, on an equal footing with others. Neither are they merely interests, or even just important or protected interests. Rights are 'interests' that have been specially entrenched in a system of justifications and thereby substantially transformed, giving them priority, in ordinary circumstances, over, for example, utilitarian calculations, mere interests, or considerations of social policy. In fact, a central function of rights is precisely to insulate right-holders from claims based on principles such as utility, which otherwise would be not only appropriate, but decisive, reasons for public or private action. This priority is not absolute — rights are 'defeasible'; in some circumstances they may be justifiably overridden — but it is essential to the way rights 'work'.

Furthermore, rights can be *claimed*. Rights/titles provide a warrant for making and pressing claims that have the special force of trumps. While one may claim that something *is* right — 'That's not the right thing to do' is a very important type of claim in moral discourse — claims of righteousness are quite different in force and function from rights-claims.

'That's wrong' ('That's not right') is more like a claim of knowledge — compare 'That's not the right answer' — even though it is a moral claim made to influence behaviour. For example, both share the characteristic use of the verb 'to be', reflecting their primary reference to standards of rectitude, whether moral or factual; what is claimed is (lack of) conformity with established standards, and this (lack of) conformity is the source of the claim's force.

'I have a right to that' is more thoroughly and immediately performative. While on its surface 'informational', such a rights — claim is a demand for action that initiates a regularised process or social practice for bringing about the duty-bearer's compliance. As Feinberg (1980:150) puts it, claiming a right *makes things happen*, and making a claim is essential to many of the most important uses of rights. This brings us back to the fundamental fact of *having* a right: a right is held by a person, who is entitled to assert or otherwise exercise it, thereby bringing his entitlement into play and controlling the development of the relationship with the duty-bearer.

In many instances, something will be right in both senses. For example, if you owe me £10, I have a right to receive £10 from you and the right thing for you to do is to repay me. The two senses may even be genetically linked. For example, the contractual conferral of rights usually will make a morally indifferent act right in the sense of 'what is right'. Conversely, social welfare programmes often seem to have emerged when certain benefits, protections or services came to be seen to be so right that they demanded that rights/entitlements be created.

In many instances, though, there is a fundamental disjunction between the two senses. For example, it may not be right to respect a right established by an unjust law. Such disjunctions are especially interesting and important to us here.

Simply because *x is* right it does not necessarily follow that anyone *has* a right to *x*. For example, even if it is right to perform acts of benevolence, such as assisting the needy and hungry, a hungry person does not, *ipso facto*, have a right to receive food from me, or from anyone else. He is not thereby entitled to my food or my money to buy food: it is my food and my money; *I* have a right to it. Therefore, we stand in quite a different relationship than we would if he had a right to receive food from me. I have duties to him but he has no rights against me.

Given that this is a book about *human* rights, one obvious reaction to this example is that it ignores the (human) right to food. In one sense this is true: the example is defined without human rights in mind, but rather in order to illustrate the disjunction between what is right and rights. In another sense, though, human rights are not being ignored, or at least not in a way that significantly alters the case. As I will argue below, human rights are held, or at least exercised, primarily in relation to the state. Therefore, they would enter into the personal relationship in this example only indirectly if at all (primarily as a critique of the regime that allows or establishes the distribution of legal rights postulated in this example). However, until the end of Chapter 2 my focus will be on the nature of rights of all types, rather than the special features of human rights.

I do not wish to deny that there are unusual circumstances where we might say that someone is morally entitled (has a right) to my food on the basis of extreme need (which can be taken to establish duties in the sense of 'what is right'). The classic example of a hungry man 'stealing' bread for his family comes immediately to mind; or, imagine a fat, rich man ostentatiously devouring a succulent roast chicken in front of a hungry crowd — although even these examples seem to me to involve excuses for violating rights more than the creation of rights solely on the basis of needs. Ordinarily, however, the fact that x is right does not imply that anyone has a right to x; mere righteousness does not entail the possession of rights.

A simple example illustrates many of the important practical differences between the two senses of 'right'. A jogger turns a corner and comes upon an elderly man being robbed and beaten. Shocked and fearful, the jogger stands, unnoticed, behind the mugger.

The victim of the assault has rights to his personal liberty and property, which are being viciously violated. The mugger has violated the victim's rights, has broken the law, and is guilty of moral crimes as well. Thus he has failed to discharge the obligations arising from both senses of 'right'. The jogger's position, however, is substantially more complex. The right thing for him to do is to assist the victim, but this obligation is largely independent of the victim's rights, which will have been adequately respected simply by not interfering with his personal liberty or bodily integrity.[1]

The victim needs, hopes for, and on the basis of what is right deserves, and may even expect, assistance. However, he cannot demand it *as his right* (in the sense of 'having a right'). His right to personal liberty obliges others not to interfere with him, but requires nothing more than non-interference; while he *deserves* help, he is *entitled* only to non-interference.[2]

The differing sources of obligation and the resultant differences in the relationships between the parties — i.e. the different senses of 'right' involved — therefore have major consequences. The victim is specially entitled to his personal liberty and can demand, as his right, that he be left alone. He also may press special claims for relief or reparation. While of little comfort at the time of the attack, these additional protections are of considerable general, long-run value to him and to other right-holders.

The victim's appeals to the jogger, though, are merely appeals. If the jogger fails to live up to his obligation to aid the old man he is subject (only) to moral condemnation. Furthermore, this condemnation will be of a different sort from that applied to the mugger, for the jogger has given the victim everything to which he is entitled. This is not to say that moral indignation is unimportant or insignificant — consider our judgements of those dozens of people who watched or heard Kitty Genovese being murdered and did absolutely nothing to help — but our judgements do differ substantially.

Rights provide special protections, create special obligations, and place their possessors in a special position in seeking to obtain that to which they are entitled. Often, though, they are limited in scope compared to right in the sense of 'what is right'. It cannot be determined, apart from particular cases, which protections and obligations are likely to be more efficacious. However, what we can expect from others, what they are obliged to do in relation to us, what they are at liberty to do or not as they choose, all depend in large measure on the sense of 'right' involved.

In the next chapter we will consider the nature of rights in more detail. Before that, let me make a few comments on the 'human' part of 'human rights'. The definitional issues here involve the *source* of human rights (rather than their character as rights) and the ways in which *human* rights differ from other rights (rather than from what is right).

Not all the rights held by human beings are 'human rights'; for example, contractual and constitutional rights are held by humans but are not 'human rights'. Human rights are those held simply by virtue of being a person. To have a human right one need not be or do anything special, other than be born a human being.[3]

In an older idiom, human rights are *natural* rights, rights held on the basis of one's nature as a human being.[4] But how can 'nature' give rise to rights? Rights generally are classified by their source: e.g. legal rights are established by the law, contractual rights by contracts, and thus, apparently, natural rights by nature. But while laws and contracts invest persons with rights through rather clear and well-established mechanisms, 'nature' would seem to be incapable of bestowing rights. Furthermore, although everyone has a human nature, not everyone is able to enjoy the rights it gives rise to; man thus would seem to take away what nature 'gives'. But this is puzzling, for not only are natural rights the highest class of rights, and thus seemingly relatively immune to cancellation by human decision, but the human actions that 'take away' rights do not — cannot — take away the human nature that supposedly gives rise to them.

The language of 'human rights' can help to clarify matters. If human rights are the rights one has simply as a human being, then by 'human being' we mean much more than a creature of a particular species and genus. Human rights are the rights of *man* — not *Homo sapiens* or 'man' the featherless biped, but rather 'man' the *zoon logon ekhon, zoon politikon, animale rationalis*; a true *human* being; the Yiddish *mensch*. The 'nature' which underlies natural or human rights is the *moral* nature of a human being. Society may develop or thwart this nature, and laws may respect or repress it, but it is essential to, and cannot be taken from, man. This conception will be developed in much more detail in Chapter 3.

Since all human beings 'have' the same basic nature and have it 'equally', the rights based on this nature must be universal and held equally by all. Human rights are also universal rights in the further sense that they hold against all men and institutions; they are what jurists call rights *in rem* — i.e. rights to some 'thing', which therefore place obligation on people in a position to deny or violate them — rather than rights *in personam*, which hold only against a special class of persons. Because human tights are essential to a life worthy of a human being, no one can be left unobliged by them.

Our subject, then, is those universal rights/titles held equally by all persons simply because they are human beings. Our goal in what follows is to specify in some detail how these rights function and their theoretical foundations; i.e. to begin to develop a theory of human rights.

Notes

1. While this conceptualisation of the victim's rights as 'negative' rights — rights that impose only duties to abstain from interfering — is contentious, it does seem to me to be the way in which virtually all societies of which I am aware conceive such rights *as they hold against other citizens*; the 'positive' duties correlative to these rights are largely directed to the state. Once more, my point is simply that, as such a case is ordinarily conceived, there is an important practical difference between x being right and A having a right to x, and the former does not entail the latter (which has important implications for human rights, as we shall see below).

2. For completeness we can note that the mugger has few rights which enter into his relationship with the victim or the jogger. However, if they overpowered him and then proceeded to injure or kill him, after he had ceased to resist, we would probably say that his rights had been violated — perhaps understandably, but violated none the less. The victim and the jogger are obliged by his legal and human rights to use only that force necessary for self-defence and to leave retribution to the legally constituted authorities, regardless of what he 'deserves'.

3. I am ignoring any differences between 'person' and 'human being'. However, for an illustration of the importance of this distinction in certain extreme cases, see Morris 1981.

4. There are subtle differences in emphasis between 'human rights', 'natural rights' and 'the rights of man'. However, for most purposes these can be ignored (although the justification for this claim lies largely in the adequacy of the following analysis, which treats the contemporary notion of human rights as an extension of more traditional natural rights ideas). For an argument that a natural rights conception can encompass the full range of internationally recognised human rights, see Donnelly 1982b.

2 THE NATURE OF (HUMAN) RIGHTS: 'HAVING' A HUMAN RIGHT

Rights as a Practice

What 'is' a right? The simplest answer to this question was provided by Bentham, who argued that rights are merely beneficial obligations. 'It is by imposing obligations, or by abstaining from imposing them, that rights are established or granted.' 'To assure to individuals the possession of a certain good, is to confer *a right* upon them.' (1838:III, 181, 159; compare 1970:221n, 271; 1838:III, 217, 221; 1931:93; 1928:97.) I shall call this the 'simple beneficiary theory' of rights: being the intended beneficiary of an obligation is a necessary and sufficient condition for the possession of a right; A's right *is* B's obligation to render some beneficial service to A (compare Lyons 1969; Hart 1973).

Counter-examples to this theory abound:

(1) I'm walking across a footbridge and see a man in the river, struggling to stay afloat. I ought to try to rescue him — I have a moral obligation at least to get help; this would be the right thing to do — but he has no right to assistance from me.
(2) My neighbour notices someone lurking outside my window at night. He has an obligation to alert me, or the police — it would be right for him to do this — but I have no right to demand that my neighbour protect my property.
(3) I have a rare type of blood needed immediately to save the life of an accident victim. While this imposes a deep moral obligation on me to give blood, the accident victim has no right to my blood.

Despite the strength of these moral obligations, in the absence of entitlement there are no rights. The duty-bearer is obliged to render a beneficial service, but should he fail to do so, he violates no rights. The beneficiary may appeal to duty and righteousness, but he cannot claim a right. Mere beneficial obligation falls far short of rights, despite the fact that rights do entail obligations, which generally are beneficial. In other words, the simple beneficiary theory confuses what is right with having a right, and thus obscures the true nature of rights.

An adequate theory of rights must start with titles and claims and the special relationships they govern between right-holders and duty-bearers. 'A has a right to x (with respect to B)' specifies a right-holder (A), an 'object' (x), and a duty-bearer (B), and indicates the relationships in which they stand as a result of the right. As we have seen, A is entitled to x; A's right to x is, among other things, a title to x (held with respect to B). B stands under correlative obligations to A (with respect to x) and, should it be necessary, A may make special claims upon B to discharge these obligations. These claims are based on A's title, while that title is of value primarily because it grounds such claims.

As a title, the right governs the relationship between right-holder and duty-bearer (in so far as that relationship depends on rights). As a claim, the right places the right-holder in direct control of that relationship; the duties correlative to rights 'belong to' the right-holder, who is largely free to dispose of them as he sees fit (compare Hart 1973). In both aspects the relational character of rights is crucial: one has a right *to* something *with respect to* certain persons.

Titles point from the right-holder towards the object of the right. Claims also point, towards those obliged by the right, in relation to whom it is held. Rights thus create a 'field' of rule-governed inter-actions centred on the right-holder. 'Having a right' is less holding something than standing in a special, and controlling, relation to certain persons (who are bound by correlative obligations) and 'objects' (to which one is entitled). Rights 'are' more a social practice than 'things'. Therefore, we should ask how rights 'work', rather than what they 'are'. Rights are *rights*, not something else, a point underscored by focusing on the practice.

The dangers and distortions of reductionist approaches are particularly clear in the simple beneficiary theory. 'Right-holders' are reduced to objects or passive recipients of benefits, making exercise of one's right virtually impossible. Under a simple beneficiary theory one enjoys a benefit, but can hardly be said to have a right. In fact, rights become superfluous under such a theory: rights-language becomes interchangeable with duty-language; having a right collapses into what is right (compare Bentham 1838:III, 159).

Unless we want to eliminate the language and behaviour particularly characteristic of rights, we must resist seeking to reduce rights to obligations — or to anything else — and instead examine the workings of the practice. If we want to understand rights, we must explore the bonds between right-holders, duty-bearers and rights-objects, the rules by which their relationships are governed, and the patterns and processes through which these relations unfold.

Exercise, Respect and Enjoyment of Rights

Consider the following simple model. A right-holder *exercises* his right, in the generic sense of bringing it into play. This activates the duty-bearer's obligation to *respect* the right. If it is respected, the right-holder can be said to *enjoy* his right. The result of this process, and its ultimate aim, is the right-holder's enjoyment of the *object* of his right.

As simple as this model seems, it is too robust for most actual transactions between right-holders and duty-bearers. For example, if I buy a suit I have a right to the money in my wallet when I enter the store, and a right to the suit when I leave. None the less, despite the fact that right-holders and duty-bearers interact in connection with rights-objects, this transaction is seriously misrepresented as a rights transaction. While it would be wrong to say, for example, that I don't have a right to spend my money on a suit, it would be equally wrong to *say* that I do — barring very unusual circumstances, it would be pointless, silly, or worse. Phenomenologically, my rights are not part of the transaction, either for me or for the salesman, who no more respects my rights than I exercise them. It is even misleading to speak of enjoying rights here: if I 'enjoy' anything it is the *objects* of my rights (my money and the suit), not my rights.

Talk of rights is sensible and appropriate only when rights are in some way at issue. For example, if A has a contract to deliver parts to B's assembly plant, their transactions usually will involve 'business as usual' rather than the exercise, respect and enjoyment of rights. But if A puts his factory on overtime to meet his delivery deadline out of respect for B's rights, then we not only can, but probably should, speak of B enjoying his rights. But despite A's active respect of B's rights, no rights have been *exercised*.

We can begin, then, by distinguishing three basic processes:

(1) 'assertive exercise', involving the 'full' three-step process of exercise, respect and enjoyment;

(2) 'direct enjoyment', as in the contract involving overtime, in which the duty-bearer forms or alters his behaviour in light of the right, so that we can speak of the right being respected and enjoyed, but not exercised; and

(3) 'objective enjoyment', as in the purchase of the suit, in which the *object* of the right is enjoyed, but the right is not exercised, respected or enjoyed.

I choose the term 'assertive exercise' to stress the making of a claim and the active pursuit by the right-holder of the enjoyment of the right and its object. 'Enjoyment', by contrast, suggests a relatively passive role for the right-holder.[1] The terms direct and objective enjoyment are a bit awkward, but they do highlight important elements of such transactions. 'Direct enjoyment' stresses the right-holder's enjoyment of the right without the mediation of a claim. 'Objective enjoyment' underscores the fact that only the object of the right is enjoyed. Furthermore, since the right does not directly enter into a transaction that results in objective enjoyment, only an 'objective' outside observer with a special analytic purpose would speak of the transaction as involving rights.

This considerable variety in the way rights work — and we have only begun to chart it — reflects the complexity of social practices. Following Wittgenstein's remarks on 'regions of language' (1958:para. 18, 90; compare Pitkin 1972:140–9) we can speak of regions in the practice of rights. Wittgenstein compares a natural language to an ancient city, with a maze-like, irregular plan. As we are beginning to see, this is very much like the practice of rights. Such a city/practice is divided into districts or sub-regions, which can be mapped. This 'mapping' is one of my primary objectives here. And much as the later Wittgenstein stressed practice-oriented notions such as 'language games' and 'family resemblances', in opposition to his earlier picture theory and other single-factor and reductionist views, my stress on rights as a social practice is intended to emphasise the complexity and variety of rights.[2]

Thus it is important to stress that objective and direct enjoyment are perfectly standard processes, or 'regions', in the practice of rights. In fact, they are, and must be, the norm. The claiming that characterises assertive exercise reflects the right-holder's perception of a threat to his right or its object, and presses upon the duty-bearer his obligation, often with considerable force; even direct enjoyment may involve major costs, inconvenience, discontent or tension. If a system of rights is to survive, objective enjoyment must be the prevalent way in which rights work. 'Excessive' resort to assertive exercises is likely to eat away, even explode, the practice, by destroying the minimum social harmony without which a system of rights cannot survive. Therefore, assertive exercise is in an important sense the 'degenerate' case.

However, it also is of unparalleled importance to the right-holder, and a defining feature of rights: not only do rights really count when they don't work through direct or objective enjoyment, but the availability of assertive exercise is crucial to distinguishing rights from other practices, and from other grounds on which the same 'object' might be held. For example, a thief who steals my stereo may 'enjoy' it (or the proceeds from its sale) but he doesn't have a right to it. Likewise, I may 'enjoy' freedom of movement without a right to it; for example, others may be indifferent to my movement or may lack the power to interfere. Someone may even 'respect' my liberty or my holdings without any rights being involved, perhaps out of a sense of fairness or magnanimity, or because of a divine injunction. Unless I can claim something as my right/title, I simply enjoy a benefit, without having a right.

The availability of assertive exercise thus serves as a test of sorts for the possession of rights. But it is hardly a simple litmus test: resort to assertive exercise must be exceptional; right-holders usually are free to choose not to exercise their rights; some attempted exercises will fail and others will be (justly) overridden by other rights or even powerful non-rights demands; and so forth. *Enforcement*, however, is often argued to be just such a test.

Enforcement and Rights: The 'Possession Paradox'

To turn a phrase from Hobbes, rights without the sword are but mere words. The most prominent version of this view is the legal positivist argument that in the absence of (legal) enforcement one does not 'have' a right. As Austin puts it, 'if [the] corresponding duty be a creature of a law imperative, the right is a right properly so called' (1954:158-9; compare 11-12, 141-2). While more sophisticated contemporary legal positivists (Hart 1973; Raz 1979: Chs 14, 15) recognise moral rights and offer a legal positivist account of legal rights only, this extreme positivism is historically important, retains considerable popular appeal, and provides a useful focus for examining the place of enforcement in the practice of rights.

'Rights imply remedies' is an old and valuable legal maxim: when the simple processes considered above fail, we may move into remedial regions of the practice. For example, if the validity of one's title is questioned, or its application to the case at hand disputed, one usually can seek a 'remedy' in special regions of the practice established to resolve such disputes. In such cases both 'exercise' and 'respect' of the right are likely to centre on participation in these procedures. And if the right is infringed or violated, the right-holder usually is entitled to make claims for redress or restitution not only of the duty-bearer but of political authorities as well; i.e. one may demand that one's right be enforced.

'Having', 'enjoying' and 'enforcing' a right do go together. But they do not always go together, nor do they always combine in the same ways; in particular cases, the connection is no more necessary than that between exercise, respect and enjoyment. Therefore, simple lack of enforcement will not establish the absence of a right.

For example, if a thief steals my car and is never apprehended, I still have a right to the car, as well as a remedy in the form of the police and the courts; if the car turns up, it is still mine, and I am certainly better off with the police looking and the threat of the courts serving as a general restraint on theft. Furthermore, although unable to enjoy the object of my right (the car), I still do have a right to it and even enjoy that right, for example, in the legal remedies on which I draw.

Admittedly, both right and remedy are ineffective in this case. Furthermore, my enjoyment of the right is of dubious significance, in this instance at least. The same may be true, however, even if the right is successfully enforced. For example, if the thief is found, after smashing my car into a tree and destroying it, and then sent to jail, I will 'enjoy' my right as a result of its retributive enforcement, but without the car I remain deprived of the enjoyment of the object of my right, which was the point of having a right. *Possession* of a right, the *respect* it receives, and the ease or frequency of *enforcement* are quite separate issues.

One may have an unenforced and unenjoyable right. Enforcement may be essential to the full enjoyment of a violated right, but it is no test for possession of a right. In fact, not only objective enjoyment, but even most instances of direct enjoyment and assertive exercise have no phenomenologically significant reliance on enforcement.

The positivist might respond that a right need only be broadly enforceable, in the sense that generally appropriate enforcement mechanisms are regularly available to the right-holder. Therefore, rather than sporadic breakdowns such as theft, systematic 'breakdowns' in the enforcement of (alleged) rights provide the true test of the theory. One's title, the claims it grounds, and the correlative obligations it entails all point towards enjoyment of the right and its object, which will demand enforcement in extreme cases. If in virtually all cases in which the right is at issue it is not enjoyed, due to systematic lack of enforcement, does one really have it as a right? For example, do Soviet citizens have a right to freedom of speech?

Soviet law, the Soviet Constitution, and international treaties to which the Soviet Union is a party all recognise this right. Therefore, Soviet citizens do 'have' a right to free speech, in the sense that they have a valid (municipal and international) legal title. But should they actually claim the right, the attempted exercise is likely to be frustrated by law and policy. Therefore, Soviet citizens don't 'have' a right to freedom of speech, in the sense of being able to enjoy it; their title is valid but not effective. And yet the fact that dissidents and human rights activists *do* 'have' this right/title is what makes them such an embarrassment; they are entitled to do what they are punished for doing — and everyone knows it.

I shall call this 'the possession paradox': 'having' and 'not having' a right at the same time, and the 'having' being particularly important precisely when one doesn't 'have' it. This possession paradox is central to the practice of rights, and particularly characteristic of human rights. In many important cases, talk of having systematically unenforced rights is not only coherent, but necessary.

Even in the case of legal rights, the positivist account breaks down. Consider the constitutional civil rights of American Blacks, which received little enforcement even as late as the fifties and sixties. Because of the lack of enforcement, positivists would argue that Blacks did not have these rights and that their protests were aimed at obtaining new rights. But American courts found, and continue to hold, that all Americans did (and do) 'have' such rights; minorities were ('only') systematically deprived of their enjoyment.

Voting rights, due process and equal protection, even in the forties and fifties, were rights — titles grounding valid rights-claims

— not just desirable goals of social policy. Civil rights advocates and protesters were not just another special interest group; they weren't even just social reformers pressing claims of moral righteousness. Rather, they were demanding that the constitutional rights of minorities be protected and enforced. The issue was one of enforcing, not creating, rights.

Compare this with the struggle for 'welfare rights'. Food stamps, for example, could be claimed to be humane, just, equitable, or politically expedient, but prior to congressional legislation one could say only that poor people ought to be given a (legal) right to food stamps, not that they had one. Such claims do have considerable moral and political force, but they concern what a just society ought to provide, rather than the rights people have and the resultant duties of the government.

It is even misleading to say that the lack of legal enforcement made the civil rights of Blacks defective. Their (constitutional) title was not defective; the appropriate analogy is not an improperly registered deed or an incorrectly staked mineral claim. Neither were their claims defectively asserted; the proper analogy is not failure to meet a filing deadline or bringing suit under the wrong provisions of a statute. Blacks did have a valid title and they did advance valid rights-claims. Their problems lay not so much in their rights/titles/claims as in recalcitrant political institutions. Yet because these rights were not protected or effectively guaranteed by the authorities, they were, in a sense, defective — and the civil rights movement was directed to remedying these defects.

In a certain sense, American Blacks in Alabama in 1950 did not 'have' a (legal) right to equal protection of the laws; they had not received, and they continued to be denied, equal protection. But in an equally important sense they *did* 'have' such a right; *all* Americans have it. An adequate analysis of rights must be able to capture the full complexity of this possession paradox.

If Blacks simply didn't have the right, then when, how and from where did they get it? Positivists would seem to be forced back to arguments of judicial legislation. Such arguments, however, are not only morally and juristically dubious, they are entirely superfluous — the right already was in the Constitution and did not need to be created.

But if Blacks had the right all along, what was all the fuss about? Things *are* seriously amiss when a legal right goes systematically unenforced; while 'only' enforcement was missing, enforcement is so important to the practice, and in this case was missing to such a degree, that possession of the right had become 'paradoxical'.

How can we account for the changes which did take place without denying the reality of either the right or its defects prior to these changes? Following Dworkin (1977:134–6; compare Pitkin 1972:186–92) we can suggest that the 'conception' of the 'concept' changed; i.e. our understanding of the concept of 'equal protection' developed as a result of a more thoughtful consideration of its meaning, scope and practical implications. Courts, rather than create rights, give voice to, record, or validate the authoritative 'conception' of a right; even at this level we have a 'finding' of the court. And rights-claims made an important contribution to the transformation of the political standing of the civil rights of Blacks, who used their rights, in the sense in which they did have them, in order to vindicate those rights, which in an equally important sense they did not have.

This analysis is very much in line with, for example, Chief Justice Warren's decision in *Brown v. Board of Education of Topeka* (347 US 483 [1954]): 'The plaintiffs contend that segregated public schools are not "equal" and cannot be made "equal", and that hence they are deprived of equal protection of the laws.' The issue was not whether Blacks had a right to equal protection — even fringe groups rarely denied that Blacks *had* a right to equal protection — but the extent and implications of the right. Furthermore, Warren's decision rested on the impact of changes in American society on our 'conception' of equal protection; as the decision puts it, on a consideration of 'public education in the light of its full development and its present place in American life throughout the nation.'

The positivist response that *Brown* created a new right to integrated public education is, at best, extremely misleading; what was genuinely new was the inference that 'equal protection' included integrated education. None the less, it would be equally misleading to say, without qualification, that American Blacks 'had' the same constitutional rights in the forties as they have today — and not just because of the 24th Amendment prohibiting poll taxes, which traditionally had been used to discriminate against Blacks. They did, but then again they didn't; or at least they didn't *enjoy* the same rights, in the same way — because of a lack of enforcement.

Whereas the civil rights of Whites (or at least most white males) usually received objective or direct enjoyment, Blacks could count on many of their basic civil rights being overlooked or violated. Therefore, they were forced to resort not only to assertive exercises, but to a relatively frequent use of remedial exercises. But while occasioned by systematic non-enforcement — i.e. by the fact that they didn't 'have' (equal) civil rights — these exercises underscored the important sense in which they did 'have' these rights; Blacks used their rights to gain those same rights.

A similar argument can be made for rights such as freedom of speech in the Soviet Union. Soviet dissidents can and do appeal to their constitution, much as American Blacks did. They appeal as well to international human rights treaties ratified by the USSR, especially Article 19 of the *International Convenant on Civil and Political Rights.* Furthermore, the situation is generally perceived, by participants and observers alike, to involve questions of enforcement, not possession, of the right. Dissidents present their cases as involving violations of rights, both legal and human. Public outcry and discussion in the West centres on the violation of rights, particularly internationally recognised human rights. Even the Soviet authorities only deny that they are *violating* these rights; they too argue that Soviet citizens have them.

If this is merely the compliment of vice to virtue, it is a compliment with powerful theoretical implications — and it is hard to dismiss all of this as self-serving talk, in light of the fact that governments and the public alike in both the US and the USSR seem to have come to the same conclusions. There are well-established legal and moral rules, practices and principles that validate the claims of Soviet citizens to have a right to freedom of speech, both as citizens and as human beings. But while their title is good, their claims tend to be (legally) ineffective, leaving us again with a clear case of systematically unenforced rights. The difference between the American and Soviet cases is one of the relative success or failure of attempted exercises of rights.

Special Features of Human Rights

In both of these examples, several kinds of rights entitled the right-holder to the object in question; for example, Soviet citizens could claim municipal legal, constitutional, international legal, moral and human rights to free speech. But while American Blacks generally used constitutional rights in their struggle, Soviet dissidents have made relatively frequent use of human rights claims. The reasons for this highlight some of the distinguishing features of human rights.

If A can claim x on the basis of two or more kinds of rights, his preference usually will be for the 'lowest' available right that shows reasonable promise of securing enjoyment of x. For example, rather than claim a human right to freedom of speech or assembly, most Americans will use the 'lower' constitutional right, and an even lower right would be still more desirable (e.g. a prior contract to use a meeting hall, or a town ordinance governing the issuance of march permits). The reason for this, of course, is that 'lower' rights tend to be more readily enforceable or easier to use.

Ease of use or enforcement, however, is not equivalent to possession. In fact, the special functions of human rights almost *require* that human rights be unenforceable.

An appeal to human rights is testimony to the absence of enforceable positive rights. For example, American gays must claim human rights because even constitutional rights provide few protections against discrimination on the basis of sexual preference. One *claims* a right only when its enjoyment is threatened or denied. Therefore, the existence of an enforceable 'lower' right to the 'same' thing leaves the higher right without a use — for the moment.

All rights claims are a sort of 'last resort': rights are actually claimed only when one doesn't 'have' the right (in the sense that it is not receiving direct or objective enjoyment) or fears that it cannot be enjoyed without assertive exercise. Claims of human rights in turn are the final resort in the realm of rights; there is no higher rights appeal available. They also are likely to be a last resort in the sense of 'I've tried everything else and while maybe not much will come out of this . . .' Unless other rights-based remedies have been exhausted, one usually will not resort to human rights claims. Therefore, the possession paradox, simultaneously 'having' and 'not having' a right, is especially characteristic of human rights, because claims of human rights, by their very nature, rarely will be legally enforceable.

This extralegality implies that the primary use of human rights will be to change existing institutions. For example, Soviet dissidents press their human rights claims in order to alter the

standard practice of the Soviet state. Therefore, the close connection between natural rights ideas and, for example, the French
Revolution, is characteristic rather than accidental. If systematically
unenforced rights are to be enforced and enjoyed, institutions must
be transformed. This is true of all rights — consider, for example,
the widespread changes brought about by the American civil rights
movement — but the 'higher' the right, the greater the likely change.

Major institutional change, however, may arise from many
sources. Rights-based social change is distinguished by the prior
entitlement of the right-holder, with the special force this gives to his
claims, and by the fact that the right-holder uses his right to remove
the barriers to its enjoyment. Systematically unenforced rights position the right-holder to mount a particularly powerful attack on the
institutions that deny him his rights. This is why having even an
unenforced right is so important.

The transforming role of human rights implies that human rights
claims aim to be self-liquidating. One of the underlying purposes of
human rights claims is to establish, or to bring about greater
enforcement of, a parallel 'lower' right; for example, the civil rights
movement aimed to bring legal practice into accord with the constitutional requirements of equal protection. To the extent that such
claims are effective, the need to make them is eliminated; one continues to have the right, but there is no need or occasion to *use* it. All
rights claims can be viewed as aiming to be self-liquidating — this is
just another aspect of the possession paradox and the importance of
direct enjoyment to the practice — but it is particularly characteristic of human rights.

Thus the primary political functions of human rights, once we
move from opposition to positive action, are likely to lie in the
guidance they provide in founding a regime or revising its basic
structure. Within the natural or human rights tradition society and
government are seen as collective instruments for establishing
parallel 'lower' rights in order to secure the enjoyment of natural
rights. For example, the French *Declaration of the Rights of Man
and the Citizen* declares that 'the end of all political association is
the preservation of the natural and imprescriptible rights of man';
and Mackintosh (1792:110) argues that 'the first duty of law-givers
and magistrates is to assert and protect' the equal natural rights of
man. In other words, human rights provide a standard of legitimacy
for any government (see, e.g., Paine 1945:I, 5, 276–7; Wollstonecraft

1795:7; Locke 1967:para. 95; and Bay 1968:241). But in a legitimate government so defined, actual claims of human rights will be rare; in a properly constructed regime, human rights provide guidance at the founding, and are occasionally claimed in order to remedy deviations from founding principles, but otherwise do not play an active political role.

Paine goes so far as to argue that every civil right is merely 'a natural right exchanged', and that in this exchange society grants one nothing (Paine 1945:I, 276; compare Wollstonecraft 1795:406). This suggests that there is no essential difference between civil and natural rights. In fact, though, human rights are substantially transformed in the 'exchange' — not in their substance, but in the way they work. In particular, their enforcement becomes public, regularised and more secure. While the substance of the claims based on parallel civil and natural rights may remain the same, the avenues available to the right-holder in pursuit of enjoyment of the rights will be quite different. The legal positivist analysis correctly emphasises this point, but distorts it by turning it into a test for the possession of a right.

Paine tries to reduce civil rights to natural rights. Legal positivists attempt a different sort of reduction, insisting on a legal model of rights that makes 'human rights' at best defective or merely protorights. In each case, though, the error arises from an attempt to impose a single, simple model of rights on a complex practice of multiple processes or 'regions'. Misplaced legal analogies, however, present a particularly serious threat in contemporary analyses, especially when considering the special reference of human rights to political institutions and their use in bringing about social change.

For example, Feinberg (1980:153) argues that human rights are rights only in a 'manifesto sense', an argument that has been picked up by Beitz (1979:56), among others. This conception, however, degrades human rights, apparently as a result of a misplaced legal model of rights. As the term has come to be used, to claim a 'manifesto right' is to claim that x ought to be recognised as a right, without qualification, even though it is not a valid right at the moment. A 'manifesto right', however, is not a right at all: one is neither entitled to anything nor can one advance rights-claims on the basis of such a 'right'. A 'manifesto right' is merely a demand for rights, a particularly insistent 'ought'. But while human rights do imply a manifesto for political change, that does not make them any less truly rights. Rather, it underscores the fact that they are human rights, not legal rights.

Similarly, Rex Martin (1980:396) argues that

> insofar as human rights claims are addressed principally to governments, we have to regard practices of governmental recognition and promotion as included within the notion of human rights . . . the right is the claim *as* recognized in law and maintained by governmental action.

Without legal recognition we may have morally valid claims, but not human *rights*. Legal recognition and government protection, according to Martin, 'serve to constitute the claim a right' (1980:402).

While correctly emphasising the special reference of human rights to governments, Martin misconstrues the nature of human rights claims against governments. He quotes Hart in support of his position — 'men speak of their moral rights mainly when advocating their incorporation into the legal system' (Hart 1955:177) — but then ignores the crucial element of the demand for incorporation, a demand that would be incoherent if the right already were a legal right. As a result, Martin fails to capture the special role of human rights claims of aiming to transform existing institutions and establish *new* legal rights. Most claims of human rights do have a special reference to government, but that does not mean that human rights are or must be legal rights.

Like other reductionists, Martin leaves us ultimately without recognisable human rights. Consider his claim that 'In a society which has no civil rights (e.g. a caste society, in particular one with a slave caste) there are no human rights. They are not observed there' (1980:401). The first sentence, as a sociological claim about the political rights enjoyed in these societies, is likely to be true. As a conceptual point, however, it is of little or no significance, unless we assume that people have only those rights the state says they have, an assumption that makes nonsense of most claims and discussions of human rights. The problem, as the second sentence indicates, is that Martin confuses *having* a right with *enjoying* it or having it *respected*.

If we permit this collapsing of categories, the state becomes the *source* of human rights and we end up denying the existence of human rights, the rights of man as opposed to the rights of the citizen.

We also strip human rights of their universality and make the very notion of universal human rights incoherent, except under a single world government. Universality, however, has been a central element of the tradition from Locke right up to the *Universal Declaration of Human Rights* and the *International Human Rights Covenants*. Martin in effect reduces human rights to constitutional rights, which forces us to deny either that there are human rights or that human rights are true rights. Either is in conflict with our language, behaviour and political practice.

Human rights differ in significant ways from legal rights. This is hardly surprising: different kinds of rights have different features and perform different functions, which is why it is useful to have more than one type. Both legal and human rights work as rights — titles that ground rights-claims — despite distinctive variations in their operation. These differences, without a doubt, centre on legal enforcement. This is not surprising either, since legal rights are defined by their recognition in law.

We must resist even the suggestion that positivist analyses highlight an essential defect or weakness in human rights (Martin 1980:393), a suggestion which usually is based on an inappropriate legal model of rights. As we have seen, lack of enforcement is in many ways less a weakness of human rights than a distinguishing feature of the situations in which they are claimed. And they are 'weaker' than positive rights only in terms of enforceability; their *moral* force, for example, usually is stronger. In fact, a major strength and value of human rights is their availability when parallel positive rights are lacking. As we have seen, their primary uses depend largely on the fact that they are not enforced.

There is no single pattern in which rights work and no single feature that defines them. Even titles and claims, the organising criteria on which we have relied here, are little more than a convenient shorthand for the complex rules and relationships of the practice of rights, some of which have already been discussed above. To have a right, if it 'is' anything, is to be a right-holder, with all that this implies. It is to stand in a special relation to duty-bearers and rights-objects, and in a position to do many different things, as the case may require, and as the particular right may allow.

Notes

1. Thus one might want to suggest that Bentham's simple beneficiary theory is more incomplete than incorrect. Even this interpretation, however, is seriously misleading, for it overlooks the important connections between the parts of the practice: the individual parts are not discrete units, but rather affect one another in their interactions. For example, the process of direct enjoyment may be substantially influenced by the availability of assertive exercises. Therefore, even enjoying a right involves more than being the beneficiary of someone else's obligations.

2. This analogy is suggestive, but I do not want to push it too far. While a social practice 'is', among other things, a language region — especially in the case of a practice such as rights, in which the language-based activity of claiming is so important — it is the analogy between language and rights viewed as practices that is most important to my argument.

3 THE SOURCE OF HUMAN RIGHTS: HUMAN NATURE AND HUMAN RIGHTS

We turn now from the first theoretical level, the nature of (human) rights, to the second, the question of their source. The very term 'human rights' points clearly to their source: humanity, human nature, being a person or human being. Just as legal rights have the law as their source, and contractual rights arise from contracts, 'humanity', 'human nature', or some such aspect of all persons would seem to be the source of human rights. The problem, of course, is to specify what 'human nature' means in this context, and how it gives rise to rights.

The classic theories and documents provide little illumination. Locke ultimately falls back on divine donation: God, in his infinite wisdom and mercy, grants us natural rights; they are 'natural' in the sense that they are part of our divinely ordained human nature. Paine does not even offer this much; he simply treats the existence of natural rights as self-evident. The French *Declaration*'s assertion that 'men are born, and always continue, free and equal in respect of their rights' lacks even the suggestion of a ground, while the *International Human Rights Covenants'* claim that 'these rights derive from the inherent dignity of the human person' looks more like a pious evasion than anything else.

Recently, however, it has become popular to argue that human rights are based on human *needs*. This theory has considerable initial plausibility, since human needs are an obviously important part of 'human nature'. It is also attractive because needs can be scientifically determined, at least in principle, thus largely circumventing the philosophical problem of developing a substantive theory of human nature in order to derive a list of human rights.

Human Nature, Needs and Rights

While needs theorists tend to cluster on the political left, needs theories of human rights recently have been presented in a variety of legal, social scientific, philosophical and psychological contexts.

Needs establish human rights. (Bay 1982:67)

Assuming need is reasonably strictly defined (not as equivalent to desire or wish), a basic human need logically gives rise to a right (need for food/right to an adequate diet). (Green 1981:55)

[Human rights are] norms that regulate actions by the norm-receiver relative to other human beings in general, and their need-satisfaction in particular. (Galtung and Wirak 1977:252)

It is legitimate and fruitful to regard instinctoid basic needs . . . as *rights* as well as needs. (Maslow 1970:xiii)

Human rights, in short, are statements of basic needs and interests. (Benn 1967)[1]

Of course, not all needs imply rights: for example, 'The car needs gas', 'It needs to go a little to the left', 'The sauce needs more thyme'. There also are important differences between 'need' as a noun and as a verb (McCloskey 1976:2–4). And not even everything a human being needs is a 'human need' in the intended sense: consider, for example, the 'need' for a beer on a hot afternoon, or an adolescent's 'need' for a haircut. A 'human need', in the relevant sense, is a basic need, not a mere want, desire or interest (Green 1981:55; Bay 1981:90–4; Macpherson 1977) and a universal need, which everyone 'has' simply because they are human. These requirements obviously parallel the weight and universality of human rights.

The link between basic needs and human rights in such arguments, however, almost always appears as an unsupported philosophical premise. For example, Christian Bay, the best-known needs theorist of human rights, fails to offer any sort of argument for the needs-rights link. Abraham Maslow does argue that facts about needs imply naturally determined values (1959; compare Goldstein 1940, 1959). He does not, however, even attempt to go beyond value in general — mere 'oughts' — to rights and human rights; i.e. Maslow fails to recognise the logical gap between '*x* is good for human beings' and 'there is a human right to *x*.' But even if we grant that needs are the basis of human rights, needs theories fail to offer a conception of human nature adequate to provide a foundation for human rights.

A simple operational definition of 'need' would be 'A needs *x* if and only if *x* is essential to the proper functioning of A.' Basic human needs can be defined as the minimum requisites for health and the avoidance of illness (Maslow 1955:4; Bay 1981:92, 1982:67). Problems arise, however, as soon as we try to establish a list of human needs.

The list of scientifically validated needs is both short and concrete: minimum amounts of food energy, protein, water and other nutrients, shelter, and perhaps companionship. Such needs, however, are obviously inadequate as the source of human rights, since they are concerned almost entirely with the *maintenance* of life, rather than its *quality*; the resulting list of human rights would not even support criticism of a life that was poor, nasty and brutish.

If needs are to serve as the source of human rights, the list must include 'soft' needs, based on an expansive notion of physical and psychological health and aiming at full personal development. The best-known and most widely used soft theory is that of Abraham Maslow. (For uses of Maslow's theory, see, for example, Bay 1981:97-9, 1982:242-51; Davies 1963: Chs 1, 2; Knutson 1972; Renshon 1974, 1977.)

Maslow recognises a wide range of hierarchically ordered needs, running from survival, safety, love and affection, to higher needs for 'belongingness', esteem and self-esteem, up to 'metaneeds' of truth, goodness, beauty, wholeness, aliveness, uniqueness, perfection, completion, justice, simplicity, richness, effortlessness, playfulness and self-sufficiency (1970:Ch. 4, 1971:Ch. 9). According to Maslow these are all equally needs: deprivation of *any* of them is (psycho)pathogenic, while gratification is curative, prophylactic or leads to personal growth and development, and *all* are naturally given, ' "instinctoid" needs, intrinsic capacities and potentialities' (1970:82, 1971:Appendix D).

The completeness of this list of needs, however, is purchased at the cost of their empirical status. For example, Wahba and Bridwell review two dozen studies of Maslow's needs hierarchy in the workplace and find that 'there is little research evidence to support it. . . . Some of Maslow's propositions are totally rejected, while others receive mixed and questionable support at best' (1976:212, 233; compare Landy and Trumbo 1976:296-303). Most other studies come to similar conclusions.[2] The higher needs simply are not needs in the same sense as 'hard' needs; despite Maslow's claims to the contrary, they have not been shown to be needs 'in the same sense that water and amino acids and calcium are needs' (1955:3).

In fact, Maslow's own qualifications are theoretically devastating. 'The claim is made only that it is relatively *more* ultimate, *more* universal, *more* basic than the superficial conscious desires, and makes a closer approach to common human characteristics' (1970:xiii; compare 1955:17). But most *philosophical* theories of human nature can make this claim with equal plausibility. When Maslow admits that the higher needs 'may simply be lost, and may disappear forever', and that even lower needs may lose all motivational force if higher needs achieve 'functional autonomy' (1968:171), he effectively sacrifices the universality of human nature/needs. And the admission that 'man's instinctoid tendencies, such as they are, are far weaker than cultural forces' (1970:129; compare 1971:382–8) removes the justification for the fundamental claim that (natural) needs, and natural needs alone, are (or ought to be) the basis for human rights.

In defence of Maslow, Bay writes 'I have yet to see criticism along the line that physical sustenance, safety, affection, self-esteem, and self-development are *not* prerequisites or crucial aspects of human welfare' (1968:247). This entirely misses the point. Even if we grant that human needs entail human rights — which Bay and Maslow have assumed rather than established — it still needs to be shown that these welfare values are *needs* and thus the basis of rights.

Bay likewise misses the point when he writes in defence of Maslow's theory that 'a simple model of man, if it is realistic and open-ended, is better than no model at all' (1968:247). The real issue is not whether Maslow has a plausible *philosophical* anthropology, but whether it can be scientifically validated. Maslow's theory turns out to be hardly more scientific, and certainly far less developed, than, say, Aquinas'. Even Bay admits that 'it is premature to speak of *any* empirically established needs beyond sustenance and safety.' (1977:17; compare Galtung nd:17). I would add only that 'premature' seems excessively generous.

'Soft'-needs theories founder on scientism and false objectivism. Even leaving aside the alleged problems of inferring values from facts, Maslow-like needs theories ultimately fail because they simply are not scientific theories and yet have based themselves on their alleged empiricism. Furthermore, if we insist on needs as the basis of human rights and yet are unable to establish an adequate list of needs, human rights advocates are likely to be crippled by needs theories rather than helped. This is a danger to which Bay seems curiously oblivious.

Rather than search for a scientific dodge in the form of needs, we must directly confront the philosophical problems of a theory of the source of human rights.

A 'Constructivist' Theory of Human Rights

I shall argue that the source of human rights is man's *moral* nature, which is only loosely linked to the 'human nature' of basic human needs. Human rights are 'needed' for human *dignity*, rather than health, and violations of human rights are denials of one's *humanity* rather than deprivations of needs. We have human rights not to the requisites for health, but to those things 'needed' for a truly human life. The source of human rights must be traced back to philosophical anthropology, i.e. to a moral theory of human nature (which is what needs theories such as Maslow's ultimately amount to).

Human rights are not 'given' to man by God, nature, or the physical facts of life; to think of them in such terms is to remain tied to a vision of human rights as things. Like other social practices, human rights arise from human action. Human rights represent the choice of a particular moral vision of human potentiality and the institutions for realising that vision.

The human 'nature' that grounds human rights is a moral posit, an essentially moral account of human possibilities. While not unrelated to the human nature studied by scientists, the relation is primarily negative: the scientist's human nature sets the 'natural' outer limits of human possibility; the moral nature that grounds human rights is a selection of one set of possibilities. The scientist's human nature says beyond this we cannot go. The moral nature that is the source of human rights says that beneath this we cannot permit ourselves to fall.

As was noted above, natural or human rights theorists have always viewed government as an instrument for the protection and greater realisation (enjoyment) of human rights; a government is morally legitimate largely to the extent that it protects human rights (Paine 1945:I, 276–7; Locke 1967: para. 95; Bay 1981:5, 89). But a government which does in fact protect human rights will radically transform human nature.

Society plays a crucial role in determining how human potentialities will be realised. Human rights are institutions specifically devoted to the most complete possible realisation of that potential. To the extent that human rights are protected and implemented, they would *create* the envisioned person, so long as that vision lay within the limits of human possibility. Human rights aim to establish and guarantee the conditions necessary for the development of the human person envisioned in the underlying moral theory of human nature, thereby bringing into being that type of person. Such an analysis might be called a 'constructivist' theory of human rights.

Lists of human rights rest on a moral ideal expressed in terms of a philosophical anthropology. However, unlike most moral ideals, human rights provide a mechanism for realising that ideal, namely, the implementation and protection of the specified human rights. Built into the very character of human rights is a constructive interaction between moral vision and political reality in which the individual and the state form one another through the practice of (human) rights. The limits and requirements of state action are set by human nature/rights, but the state and society, guided by human rights, largely 'create' (i.e. realise) that nature. 'Human nature' is thus conventional; one's very nature is in part the result of individual and social actions. It is not, however, arbitrary: the visions of human nature compatible with a constructivist theory are limited both naturally by the psycho-biological bounds of human potential and socially by the formative capacity of institutions.

If we think of a person as one to whom moral language is appropriate, or as a creature possessed of inherent moral dignity (see Melden 1977; Goodin 1981:96–8; Adams 1982), a constructivist theory begins with, and always centres on, the person and his or her inherent dignity. Human rights establish and protect the social conditions necessary for the effective enjoyment of moral personality. However, rather than define '(moral) person' in abstract formal terms, the constructivist vision provides a rather detailed, substantive account. This account not only goes beyond 'the person' as an abstract moral category to a rather precisely specified conception of moral personality, but in its flexibility abandons any notion of the person as a fixed ontological structure.

'Human nature' thus appears as a *project*; just as an individual's 'nature' or 'character' results from the interaction of natural endowment, environmental influences, and individual action, the species (or rather society) creates its essential nature out of itself. Human rights provide a structure of social practices aimed at achieving a particular range of development of 'innate' potentials. Thus we are still talking about 'self-actualisation,' but in quite a different sense from Maslow.

All the great human rights theories and documents point beyond actual conditions of existence — beyond the 'real' in the sense of what has already been realised — to the possible, which is viewed as a deeper, human moral reality. Human rights are less about the way people 'are' than about what they might become; they are about *moral* persons, rather than natural or juridical persons. The *Universal Declaration of Human Rights*, for example, tells us little about what life is like in most countries, but rather tries to set out the minimum conditions for a dignified life worthy of a fully *human* being, requirements so basic that they must be recognised as rights/titles/claims, with all that entails.

These minimum standards are all too infrequently met; many, perhaps most, people regularly are treated as if they were less than human through the denial of their human rights. Yet this is precisely when (and perhaps even why) having human rights is so valuable — they demand the sort of social change required to bring to fruition the underlying moral vision of human nature, and they carry the full force of (moral) rights.

Thus human rights are at once a 'utopian' ideal and a realistic practice for institutionalising that ideal. Human rights doctrines say, in effect, 'Treat a person like a human being and you'll get one.' But they also say 'Here's *how* you treat someone like a human being', and proceed to enumerate a list of human rights which establish the framework within which a government must act. Should a government ask 'Why should we respect human rights?' the response must be something like 'Because these are human beings; the people you are torturing, oppressing or starving are human beings and as such are entitled to the treatment specified by human rights.'

In essence, then, human rights doctrines rest on something very much like an equation of having human rights and being human. Below I argue that modern social, economic and political conditions give this admittedly contentious view a certain practical plausibility. Here let me simply suggest that the constructive character of human rights is quite consistent with a variety of loosely 'empirical' evidence.

We can read 'There is a human right to x' as implying 'If people have and enjoy a right to x, then their lives will be fuller and more truly human in a very real and basic way.' Maslow fails to establish his higher 'needs' as needs because the evidence simply does not show that (all normal) people do strive after them and are made ill by their deprivation. But viewed as the moral source of human rights, such objectives appear as potential basic interests: if given the opportunity, through the implementation of human rights, most people, and most outside observers as well, would see the pursuit of such objectives as producing more fully realised lives of greater dignity. This is a very loosely testable proposition. My own impression is that most classic and contemporary lists of human rights seem to stand up reasonably well to such a test.

Human rights thus appear as a sort of self-fulfilling moral prophecy: 'Treat human beings like *human* beings (see attached list), and you'll get truly human, and more fully realised, persons.' (This is another side of human rights claims aiming to be self-liquidating.) If the underlying vision of human nature is sound, and if the derivation of a list of rights is sound as well, then the implementation of human rights will succeed in realising that previously ideal nature.

The relationship between human nature, human rights and political society thus is 'dialectical'. Human rights shape political society, so as to shape man, so as to realise the possibilities of human nature, which provided the basis for these rights in the first place. And without human rights, the 'real' human being is almost certain to be split — alienated or estranged — from his (moral) 'nature'.

This then helps to explain the familiar claim of the inalienability of human rights: one can no more lose one's human rights than one can lose one's human nature. As Paine puts it, 'whatever appertains to the nature of man, cannot be annihilated by man' (1945:I, 243). Even if one is 'in fact' a slave, the most brutalised of political prisoners, or starving from socially sanctioned poverty in the midst of plenty, one is *entitled* to freedom and equal respect simply as a human being, claims of human rights are demands to be treated as such, and the implementation, respect and enforcement of these rights will make one free and equal. The basis of the inalienability of human rights, which is philosophically problematic in most accounts (Van de Veer 1980), is thereby clarified: the claim of the inalienability of human rights is not one of practical impossibility but rather a claim of moral impossibility; one cannot lose such rights and live the life of a human being.

It should also be clear from this discussion that a constructivist theory nicely fits the special features of human rights identified above; the accounts presented here of the nature and source of human rights thus are complementary. For example, a forward-looking moral vision of human nature provides the basis for the social changes implicit in claims of human rights. Likewise, the intensity of the possession paradox in the case of human rights is another way of presenting the relationships between 'real' and 'ideal', between moral vision and political practice.

A constructivist theory also accounts for the tension between the alleged universality of human rights and their obvious historical particularity. Like other moral claims, claims of human rights rest on allegedly universal principles that we know to be at least partly historical products. Below I will argue that the concept of human rights is indigenous only to (one part of) the modern Western tradition of political thought. Lists of human rights are quite obviously historically specific, so much so that in recent years it has become popular to speak of successive 'generations' of human rights (Vasak 1977; Marks 1981). Yet essential to any *claim* of human rights is the alleged universality of the rights violated. Historical specificity is seen in a constructivist theory as arising from the limitations, peculiarities or advances in the particular philosophical anthropologies that give substance to human rights, while the universality of claims of human rights reflects their source in human nature.

The evolution of particular conceptions or lists of human rights is seen in the constructivist theory as the result of the reciprocal inter-action of moral conceptions and material conditions of life, medi-ated through social institutions such as rights. A particular list of human rights envisions not only an ideal person but a particular set of political threats to such a person. If the moral vision remains constant, the list may evolve as material conditions change (or are perceived to change) or in response to omissions or unintended consequences that become apparent as a result of the operation of the rights. The underlying moral vision may also evolve, perhaps in response to past failure, to new horizons opened by the successful implementation of already specified rights, or to 'external' forces. Most likely, both sorts of evolutionary processes will occur together, as practical experience helps us to refine our moral con-ceptions, which none the less continue to guide practice.

But despite the constructivist theory's explicitly historical approach to the specification of lists, it retains the essential universality of human rights in at least two important senses: the rights are based on universal human potentials, and they are held by all human beings. Furthermore, the substantive elements of the theory of human nature set important bounds on, and requirements for, legitimate political action, while the associated list of human rights gives a rather determinate character to the human rights claims for social transformation. As a result, the theory's historical conventionalism is kept from degenerating into arbitrariness.

Finally, the theory is fundamentally consistent with, although clearly a contemporary revision of, the classic natural rights tradition. Locke, for example, certainly did not have such an interpretation in mind. None the less, I would suggest that a constructivist account of the source of human rights is more plausible, and certainly more developed, than Locke's, and yet still broadly consistent with his theory; it can be read largely as an explication of the 'nature' in natural rights, a philosophical problem to which Locke and his successors devoted remarkably little consideration.

It is also broadly compatible with (although quite different in emphasis from) recent efforts by, for example, Alan Gewirth (1978, 1982a) and Henry Shue (1980), to develop a theory of human rights based on basic, necessary, or primary goods; the goods they specify (e.g. security, liberty and subsistence) can be seen as representing a particular substantive philosophical anthropology. For example, Gewirth writes (1982a:5):

> all the human rights . . . have as their aim that each person have rational autonomy in the sense of being a self-controlling, self-developing agent who can relate to other persons on a basis of mutual responsibility and cooperation, in contrast to being a dependent, passive recipient to the agency of others.

In resting his theory on the requirements of human agency, Gewirth seems to believe that he has avoided substantive moral assumptions, but such passages clearly indicate the central place of philosophical anthropology in his theory.

Obviously this account of a constructivist theory is at best preliminary and fragmentary, although I am afraid it is the best I am able to offer here. Furthermore, it is an entirely conceptual or formal theory. Therefore, even if it is correct it merely lays the foundation for further, more substantive, theoretical work; in particular, it points to the pressing need for politically relevant philosophical anthropology, to provide a substantive theory of human nature to 'plug in' in order to generate philosophically defensible lists of human rights. None the less, by describing the nature of the contemporary practice of human rights, a constructivist theory would seem to provide a firm, if still partial, conceptual foundation.

Historicism, Human Nature and Human Rights

A constructivist theory of human rights can be profitably viewed as an effort to wed the historicism of a Burke or Marx with the rationalism of a Paine. Despite their hostility to the idea of natural rights, Burke and Marx provide perhaps the closest parallels to the account of human nature developed above.

Burke's opposition to natural rights, which we will consider both here and in the following chapter, was fundamental and thoroughgoing. None the less, one side of his theory of human nature is essentially 'constructivist', and can be turned back against him to defeat his arguments that natural rights theories rest on an inaccurate account of the substance of human nature and the decisive role of history in shaping it.

For Burke, government, rather than an instrument for securing natural rights, is principally a device for restraining the destructive power of the passions. Society requires that the passions be 'brought into subjection' by government, the main function of which is to 'bridle and subdue' the passions (1869:V, 133, III, 310). In the absence of such restraint, the danger is that 'in the moment of riot and in a drunken delirium from the hot spirit drawn out of the alembic of hell, which in France is now so furiously boiling, we should uncover our nakedness' (1869:III, 351); the Terror was to Burke simply raw human nature let free to run amok.

'Natural' or pre-social man, for Burke as for Hobbes, is little better than a beast, and a particularly savage beast at that. Society is necessary for true humanity, and society requires a radical break with the primordial state of nature and the renunciation of any 'natural rights' arising from that state. 'Men cannot enjoy the rights of an uncivil and civil state together' (1869:III, 310). Rather than reserve natural rights Burke, like Hobbes, argues that human nature requires that they be completely renounced on entering society (1869:III, 256, 262, 311).

If human rights are grounded in human nature, the corruption of that nature by original sin or the domination of the passions does raise serious theoretical problems. But while a direct challenge to Burke's bleak picture of human nature is unlikely to take us very far, given the notorious difficulty of resolving disputes between competing theories of human nature, an indirect response, using another side of Burke's own theory, is quite promising.

Burke, like Locke, recognises an essential bifurcation of human nature into 'good' and 'bad' sides. But while natural rights are based on human nature, there is no reason why they must aim to protect or develop all aspects of that nature indiscriminately. In fact, they are much more plausibly conceived as directed to the development of the 'good' side of human nature. A constructivist theory gives particular prominence to this purpose.

Locke, for example, clearly intended such a selective fostering of human nature. He argues that natural rights must at all times be exercised within the substantive moral limits set by natural law/reason (1967: paras 6, 135), and he recognises no natural rights based on mere appetites or passions. In effect, Locke's natural law judges original human nature and selects certain aspects for special protection by natural rights, while others are consigned to be repressed by the state and other institutions. The constructivist theory is a further development of such a line of thought.

Moral judgements of original human nature certainly are controversial.[3] However, there is no good *a priori* reason to disallow such judgements to natural rights theories, especially since Burke relies just as heavily on analogous judgements. The problems at hand seem to require that human nature be subjected to moral evaluation in the course of constructing a political regime; the real issue is not the need for such evaluation, but the basis on which it is made.

This selective fostering of original human nature is especially important and plausible if, as Burke argues, human nature is plastic as well as bifurcated. Beyond restraining the darker side of human nature, Burke argues that society, as it were, creates the good side of human nature. In an important sense, human nature itself is a social product for Burke — which sounds very much like an extreme variant of the constructivist theory. For example, Burke speaks of 'human nature — either as that nature is universal, or as it is modified by local habits and social aptitudes' (1869:IV, 206–7). The modifications of locality and experience are for Burke a part of human nature.

Man has an original, or what we might call a 'natural' nature, as well as a second, social or moral nature, which is historically evolved and culturally specific, but no less a true part of 'human nature'.

> Man, in his moral nature, becomes, in his progress through life, a creature of habits, and of sentiments growing out of them. These form our second nature, as inhabitants of the country and members of the society in which Providence has placed us. (1869:XII, 164)

It is in this 'second nature' that the creative humanising work of society is reflected and natural human potential realised.

From this perspective, Burke's objection to natural rights doctrines, and the radical political reform they imply, is that they ignore the social nature of man, which is specific to individual societies, in favour of an abstract universal nature. Once man enters society human nature itself changes — and so must any rights based on that nature. But this historical variability does not make all talk of universal and inalienable natural rights nonsense. In fact, the malleability of human nature lies at the heart of a constructivist theory.

If human nature is fixed, original sin and its secular analogues present a most serious political problem. An essentially plastic nature, however, directs our attention to the more manageable question of how man is formed by history and society, and how we can intervene in this process. Thus the very bifurcation of human nature, on which Burke places so much emphasis, can be seen as a largely social product, and in particular a consequence of societies structured around inequality rather than the equal rights of man. A constructivist theory emphasises the role of politics in the determination of the modal forms for the realisation of human potentialities.

Such an approach is evident even in late-eighteenth-century natural rights theorists. For example, Wollstonecraft argues that all of society is corrupted by inequality and unnatural distinctions of rank (1795:19, 36, 47, 135, 137, 213, 247, 252, 305–6, 485, 509–12; 1791:53, 102–4; 1967:126, 136, 221–2). Societies organised around principles other than the rights of man render all established courses of action either deadends or destructive of human values. Paine also argues that institutionalised inequality — i.e. government not based on natural rights — produces generalised social degradation (1945:I, 262, 267, 289, 359, 392ff.; II, 582). The remedy, of course, is social change based on natural rights, which will change the very nature of man. For example, Paine argues that a regime based on the rights of man would actually raise all of mankind to new levels by establishing an environment where all men and women could at last be free to develop their full potential (1945: I, 275, 286-9, 363).

Therefore, Burke's critics, and the constructivist theory, in an important sense place greater emphasis on (and hope in) history and experience. But despite their environmentalism, the teleological element in natural rights theories makes a biological metaphor appropriate: an animal — man — being given, by natural rights, the conditions necessary for healthy growth and development. The metaphor with which Paine closes his *Rights of Man*, of a political thaw and the coming bloom of spring, thus applies to humanity itself. The role of natural rights is to bring about this flowering.

The evolutionary aspects of such views are particularly prominent among Burke's critics. For example, Wollstonecraft presents a linear, progressive theory of history with the French Revolution ushering in the third and highest stage of development (1795:vii-viii). 'Rousseau exerts himself to prove that all *was* right originally: a crowd of authors that all *is* right now: and I, that all will *be* right' (1967:43). But despite suggestions of historical inevitability even Wollstonecraft, who comes closest to presenting a mechanistic theory of linear progress, gives prominence to the shaping of man by society and habit and views the progressive development of history as the result of social institutions working on human nature, rather than a consequence of an imminent grand design. For example, she writes that 'it is certain, that education, and the atmosphere of manners in which a character is formed, change the natural laws of humanity' (1795:132, 508-9), and she speaks of men whose minds 'instead of being cultivated, have been so warped by education, that it may require some ages to bring them back to nature' (1791:11). Clearly, human nature here is presented in essentially constructivist terms, and the proposed remedy is likewise constructivist, namely, social and political reconstruction on the basis of natural rights to prevent further corruption and to bring forth the positive potential of human nature.

Historically it is probably true that writers such as Paine and Wollstonecraft were overly naïve and at best only dimly aware of the complexity and full significance of the dynamic interaction of human rights and human nature that lies at the heart of the constructivist theory. None the less, the general compatibility of their discussions with this perspective does seem to me to provide further indirect support for the constructivist theory as a contemporary development of the natural rights tradition, and a further elucidation required by the failure of the classic theories to give sustained attention to the problem of the source of human rights.

The similarities between certain elements of Marx's thought and the constructivist theory also merit brief comment.[4] Historical materialism implies that human nature is the creation of human activity.

> Men can be distinguished from animals by consciousness, by religion or anything else you like. They themselves begin to distinguish themselves as soon as they begin to *produce* their means of subsistence . . . Th[e] mode of production . . . [is] a definite *mode of life* . . . As individuals express their life, so they are. What they are, therefore, coincides with their production. (1975:V, 31)

> The outstanding achievement of Hegel's *Phänomenologie* . . . is thus first that Hegel conceives the self-creation of man as a process . . . [and] thus grasps objective man — true, because real man — as the outcome of man's *own labor*. (1975:III, 333)

The strong element of economic determinism and the stress on labour as the essence of man clearly distinguishes Marx from the constructivist theory. None the less, the similarities are striking: 'the nature that dwells in human history . . . is man's *real* nature'; 'if man is shaped by environment, his environment must be made human' (1975:III, 304, IV, 131). And yet it is this vision of human nature and society that underlies Marx's attacks on natural rights and related notions.

> To speak . . . of natural justice . . . is nonsense. The justice of transactions between agents of production rests on the fact that these arise as natural consequences out of the production

relationships . . . This content is just whenever it corresponds, is appropriate, to the mode of production. It is unjust whenever it contradicts that mode. (1967:III, 339–40)

The so-called *rights of man*, as distinct from the *rights of the citizen*, are simply the rights of a *member of civil society*. (1975:III, 162)

Right can never be higher than the economic structure of society and its cultural development conditioned thereby. (1968:325)

Such passages, however, have little force against the constructivist theory. Like Burke, Marx is objecting primarily to the ahistorical abstractness of some natural law and natural rights doctrines, especially as those doctrines were used by bourgeois apologists; his point is that conceptions of justice have an historical basis. The constructivist theory, however, likewise rejects notions of abstract human nature and rights in favour of concrete social determinations. The difference, of course, lies in the ways these specifications are made in the two theories.

Even here, though, the similarities are arguably much greater than they may initially appear to be. Marx unquestionably held that ruling conceptions of justice, rights and the like were primarily determined by economic structure. It is a matter of considerable contention, however, whether he believed that as such they were exempt from external moral criticism. If we read the claim that right cannot be higher than economic structure as a moral or epistemological claim, Marx held a radical moral relativism and economic determinism incompatible with the sort of external criticism of institutions implied by human rights. Read as a sociological claim, however, there is no necessary conflict between the theories.

Is Marx's critique of capitalism based solely on the constraints it imposes on further economic (and thus social, political and cultural) development, or is it based as well on a semi-independent moral judgement of the destructive consequences of capitalism? In other words, is Marx's argument primarily that capitalism is obsolescent or that it is destructive of human values? Ziyad Husami (1980:60) argues that Marx measures society by a particular conception of ideal man; i.e. the type of man produced by a given set of social institutions is measured against a substantive model of human potential. Furthermore, Husami argues (1980:54 ff.) that the 'superstructure' of ideas is only conditioned, not fully determined, by the mode of production; i.e. that there is a reciprocal interaction of base and superstructure. This leaves considerable room for an important and autonomous role for conceptions of rights and justice.

Such a reading of Marx is highly controversial, but whether it is correct or not, it highlights a crucial point of comparison with the constructivist theory. Man is fundamentally formed by 'external' processes; human nature is essentially historical. The question is the extent to which human control over the relevant historical processes is possible.

Read as a simple economic determinist, Marx would deny the possibility of a constructive autonomous role for human action; even revolution would be essentially epiphenomenal. A constructivist theory of human rights (and Husami's reading of Marx) insists that relatively self-conscious and 'free' political action can be an important factor in the shaping of the basic structures of state and society (and thereby man). In other words, political institutions, and thus human nature, are subject to meaningful human control. While the moral visions that play such a crucial role in the constructivist theory are historically conditioned, this still leaves a major range of variation within which significantly different conceptions of human nature might operate. Particular conceptions of human rights represent a choice of possible futures within this range of freedom.

Marx did not advocate, or even tolerate, human rights ideas, except as a tactical move or as a partial measure to ameliorate the ravages of class-based societies. Neither do I want to imply that Marx in any way advocated rights-based institutions; quite the contrary, as we shall see below. None the less, the central elements of Marx's theory of human nature, at least under certain readings, are very much in line with the constructivist theory and therefore may be useful in further substantive work along constructivist lines.

In summary, then, we can say that the 'human nature' underlying human rights is a combination of 'natural', social, historical and moral elements. Human rights theorists are committed to denying original sin and its secular analogues, but they are able to recognise a full range of the less attractive elements in human nature — which human rights attempt to select out. While committed to holding that the passions are not so violent and obstreperous that their control requires subordinating all other political and moral considerations to their restraint, the theory does not demand a utopian optimism about human nature.

The possibility of substantial political progress and moral development, as defined by human rights, is another fundamental premise of a constructivist theory. None the less, a constructivist theory not only avoids the promise of guaranteed, inevitable progress, but clearly and strongly insists that human development is possible only through comprehensive human action coordinated by human rights.

Finally, the theory is committed to a view of human nature as conditioned, but not fully determined, by objective historical processes. In other words, the 'human nature' that underlies human rights is quintessentially human, full of frailties but also fraught with the possibility of the greatest glory. Human rights are a practical political institution for widely realising these higher potentials.

Notes

1. Compare Eide 1978:7 and Schacter 1976:10. Occasionally, 'needs' are even defined in terms of rights: 'For most purposes, we can initially define human needs, in a *minimal* sense, as that amount of food, clean water, adequate shelter, access to health services, and educational opportunities to which every person is entitled by virtue of being born' (McHale and McHale 1979:16).

2. See, for example, Berkowitz 1969 and Fitzgerald 1977. Perhaps the strongest empirical 'confirmation' is Knutson 1972, but her focus is very limited, the operationalisations are often questionable, and the evidence shows only a statistical tendency (see her Appendix C) that is open to interpretations incompatible with Maslow's theory. Indicative of recent efforts are Mathes and Edwards 1978 and Mathes 1981. These two studies, by a single author and published in a journal extremely sympathetic to Maslow, not only find evidence supporting just three of five needs tested for, but the three are not the same in the two tests and they do not include the higher and meta needs that are essential to the generation of a plausible list of human rights.

3. One of the great attractions of needs theories is their claim to sidestep such problems. But see Watt 1982:536-7 for a persuasive argument that needs theories as well must make such choices.

4. Given the contemporary cottage industry of Marxology, little I can say here about Marx will be new or decisive. My discussion, however, is intended to illuminate the constructivist theory rather than Marx.

4 HUMAN RIGHTS AND THE LIMITS OF STATE ACTION: COMPETING THEORIES AND APPROACHES

Establishing limits on the legitimate range of state action is one of the primary functions of human rights;[1] most human rights are held or exercised primarily in relation to one's own government. Human rights, however, are only one of many strategies for limiting the state. In this chapter we will briefly examine three prominent alternatives to human rights, namely, natural law, the principle of utility, and prescription. Chapter 5 will consider two further alternatives. In the course of these comparisons my concern will be both to elaborate further the nature of human rights, and to suggest some of the important political and practical advantages of human rights.

Natural Law and Natural Rights

It is widely believed that the concept of human rights emerged from the notion of natural law (Maritain 1947:64–8; Messner 1965:278, 326; Cranston 1973:7; Palumbo 1982:9, 22). It is not even uncommon to find 'natural law' used as a rough synonym for 'natural rights'. In fact, though, the two concepts are largely unrelated; natural law represents an approach to questions of political order quite different from that of natural or human rights. This is particularly clear in Aquinas' theory of natural law and right, perhaps the best developed and best known of the classic natural-law theories.

For Aquinas, a law is 'an ordinance of reason for the common good, made by him who has care of the community and promulgated' [90.4].[2] All law is encompassed within what Aquinas calls the 'eternal law' of God [93.3]. However, this eternal law is specified in two main branches, which are largely independent of one another: the 'divine law', the inspired revelation of the Bible, which deals primarily with questions of spiritual salvation; and the natural and human laws. Politics is regulated primarily by this second branch.

Man has special access to the eternal law 'through understanding

45

the Divine Commandment' [93.5]. 'This participation of the eternal law in the rational creature is called the natural law' [91.2]. But since human reason is able to grasp only certain general principles of the perfect divine reason [1a2ae, 19.10 ad 1], natural law is restricted to general precepts. Therefore, it must be supplemented by what Aquinas calls human laws — roughly, the laws of political life and practice — which are particular specifications of the general precepts of natural law.

Natural law, which is prior to and above merely human ordinances, is the only major directly accessible restraint on abuses of power that Aquinas recognises; natural law, from which the human law flows, serves as a check on the ruler and a guarantee to the ruled that justice will be observed. Therefore, Aquinas claims that human laws — and by implication all political acts — opposed to natural law are merely acts of violence [93.3 ad 2; 95.2; 96.4]. Yet because of the absence of natural or human rights in Aquinas' theory, the political consequences of this are not what the modern reader is likely to imagine.

Although all laws ought to be consistent with one another — they are just reflections of the eternal law — fallible and corrupt men are likely to make human laws which conflict with both natural and divine law. When human and higher laws diverge, which ought to be obeyed?

Aquinas' general position is that human laws are binding in conscience if the law in question is just [96.4]. Since right (*ius*) is the object of justice, and law is the written expression of right [2a2ae, 57.1 and ad 2], this is equivalent to saying that human laws are binding in conscience in so far as they are truly laws, which in turn means that they are binding in so far as they do not diverge from the natural (or divine) law. However, Aquinas' actual discussion of what we can call 'unjust laws', laws not in accord with higher justice as expressed in natural or divine law, does not follow this line of reasoning.

As we would expect, laws that contravene divine law 'must in nowise be observed' [96.4], for to obey them would risk the loss of eternal beatitude. But laws that are unjust by way of their end (they do not aim at the common good), author (they exceed the authority of the lawgiver) or form (they do not distribute burdens proportionately)[3] do not bind in conscience except 'in order to avoid scandal or disturbance, for which cause a man should even yield his right'

[96.4; compare 93.3 ad 2 and 2a2ae, 105.6 ad 3]. This exception leaves us with 'laws' that are both binding and not binding; the requirements of natural and human law conflict, yet the priority of natural law is not unambiguously maintained. Aquinas' view that there are laws which are just only with regard to specific regimes [92.1] adds a further, and quite large, set of such problematic laws.

Tyranny, which can be viewed as rule through systematically unjust laws, presents the political problem of unjust laws in its most acute form. In his most sustained discussion of tyranny, Aquinas' advice is simple, practical and cautious: if the tyrant is not too terrible, it is best not to seek to depose him, for if one fails, he is likely to become more harsh, while success risks tearing society into factions or attaching the masses to a deceitful leader who will set himself up as a new, and even more harsh, tyrant (1949: para. 44).

But intolerable tyranny does not, in itself, justify resistance. If explicit legal authority is present and if the natural law provides sufficient moral grounds, resistance would be legitimate public action (although prudential considerations might still counsel obedience). If explicit public authority is lacking, however, resistance is unjustifiable private rebellion. Due deliberation and substantive justice alone are not sufficient justification for acting against a tyrant [2a2ae, 60.2].

Whereas human rights warrant direct remedial action when they are violated, natural law alone provides no such warrant. In the absence of explicit authority to depose the tyrant, he must be endured; recourse must be had to God alone (1949: para. 51).[4] Unauthorised resistance is not only no better in kind than the acts of the tyrant, it is actually more dangerous, according to Aquinas, for it is likely to produce faction, sedition and even civil war, thereby forfeiting all the benefits of political society in the attempt to remedy a few of its contingent defects. In the end, for Aquinas, the tyrant's unjust laws oblige, while the obligation of the natural law is effectively cancelled.

From a human rights perspective, we might say that the subjects are entitled to expect that the natural law will be obeyed by their rulers; the priority of natural law over human law is their guarantee that their rights under the natural law will be protected. When Aquinas requires obedience to the tyrant, he deprives them of the protection of the natural law by abrogating its binding force and its priority over human law. Such a reading, however, is anachronistic, and seriously misleading in its claim that the subjects are *entitled* to a just rule and have rights under the natural law. In fact, such ideas are totally absent from Aquinas' political thought in general, and from his notion of natural law in particular.

In English, 'law' generally expresses obligation or duty, much in the manner of Aquinas when he derives *lex* (law) from *ligare* (to bind) [90.1]. However, Aquinas' views diverge substantially from ours in the case of 'right'.

As noted above, right (*ius*) is, for Aquinas, the good at which justice aims, and law is the written expression of right, of the just. Thus right and law are inseparably linked. Right and law, *ius* and *lex*, are not merely correlative, nor are laws simply derived from right to protect or sanction it. Right and law, for Aquinas, are two ways of looking at the same 'thing'; they are two ways of stating a duty under which one is placed by right in the sense of 'what is right'. Aquinas' *ius* encompasses only 'what is right'; it does not translate the English 'right' in its entirety. In particular, it does not include the notion of right in the sense of 'having a right'.

Natural law does not give rise to rights, but only states what is right. Thus Aquinas considers tyranny and resistance solely in terms of what is right (i.e. in accord with natural law and justice). This is completely independent of the rights of the people.

The tyrant, like all men, is obliged to obey the natural law, which states what is right. In ruling as a tyrant he fails to fulfill this obligation, but the natural law, in itself, provides insufficient grounds for political action against him. Natural law is only a standard of judgement, not a warrant to act. Natural law gives the people no *rights* to change their rulers; the claims and appeals they may make to the tyrant lack the special force of rights/titles.

Even if a people has the right to remove a tyrant, for Aquinas this is not a *natural* right. Furthermore, natural law is not the moral foundation for the action of the people against the tyrant; self-government is consistent with, but not demanded by, the natural law and 'natural right'. And even if self-government were demanded, this would provide no natural or human *rights*, given the disjunction of rights and righteousness in Aquinas' system. The foundation of a right to self-government is human and contingent, rather than natural or necessary; such a right is a political right, perhaps even an entrenched constitutional right, but most definitely a right resting on human, not natural, law.

Compare this with parallel modern conceptions of rights to national self-determination, political participation, or revolution. Such rights generally are held to be natural and universally valid. They belong to man *qua* man, and their violation warrants remedial action by the people. Such rights simply do not exist for Aquinas; neither individuals nor groups are naturally endowed with rights on the basis of which they may make entitlement-based claims against others, let alone their rulers.

Thus the requirement to endure a tyrant is not simply the result of Aquinas' views on monarchy or peculiarities introduced by his religious perspective. Rather, it rests on a view of political 'right' formulated almost entirely in terms of 'what is right', lacking the idea of natural or human rights. Any deontological system of ethics would be likely to produce such results if applied directly to politics.

The demands of natural law may be considerable, but the position of the people in a political system based on natural law, and the operation of that system, would be quite different from one based on natural or human rights. Natural law and human rights theorists may pursue similar goals, but they rely on quite different strategies for regulating relations between citizens and the state.

Much the same is true of non-Western conceptions of 'human rights'. Most writers argue that 'human rights are not a Western discovery' (Manglapus 1978:4) and that human rights are central to traditional Islamic, African and Asian cultures. In fact, though, the substantive issues discussed today in terms of human rights — life, justice, speech, religion, work, health, education, and so forth — were traditionally handled in these cultures, *as in the pre-modern West*, almost entirely in terms of duties that were neither derivative from, nor correlative to, human rights. These societies recognised that guarantees in these areas were essential to a fully human life and the realisation of inherent human dignity. They had elaborate systems of human duties that aimed to protect and realise human dignity. However, human rights were quite foreign to their approaches.

For example, numerous authors have argued that Islam provides a comprehensive system of human rights; many have even adduced detailed lists of human rights allegedly recognised and established by Islam.[5] But where such arguments are not entirely anachronistic, they confuse what is right with human rights.

For example, the scriptural passages cited by Khalid Ishaque

(1974) as establishing a 'right to protection of life', in fact are divine injunctions not to kill and to consider life as inviolable. Likewise, 'the right to justice' proves to be instead a duty of rulers to establish justice, while 'the right to freedom' is merely a duty not to (unjustly) enslave others. 'Economic rights' turn out to be duties to earn a living and help provide for the needy, and 'the right to freedom of expression' actually is an obligation to speak the truth.

There can be little objection to claims that in Islam 'it is the state's duty to enhance human dignity and alleviate conditions that hinder individuals in their efforts to achieve happiness' (Said 1980:87). It may even be plausible to argue that 'there is no aspect of human need but Islam, in its ethical, social and liturgical precepts, has made provision for it' (Tabandeh 1970:10). The social and political precepts of Islam do reflect a strong concern for human good and human dignity. But such a concern, although a prerequisite for human rights notions, is not equivalent to a concern for, or recognition of, human rights. The precepts of Islam, much like Aquinas' natural law, are concerned only with right in the sense of 'what is right'.

In much the same fashion, Dunstan M. Wai (1980:116), in order to show that 'traditional African societies supported and practiced human rights', argues that 'traditional African attitudes, beliefs, institutions, and experiences sustained the "view that certain rights should be upheld against alleged necessities of state." ' Such an argument confuses human rights with limited government. There are many bases on which a government might be limited — divine commandment, natural law, human rights, legal rights, extra-legal checks such as the balance of power, etc. Therefore, the simple fact that a people enjoys rule by a limited government says nothing about human rights. Yet Wai and others base their arguments on little more than a demonstration of the existence of established checks on government powers.

'There is no point in belaboring the concern for rights, democratic institutions, and rule of law in traditional African politics' (Wai 1980:117; compare Said 1979:65; Manglapus 1978; Pollis and Schwab 1980:xiii–xvi). While certainly true, this is largely irrelevant to a discussion of human rights, given the *form* such concerns took. Even where Africans had personal rights *vis-à-vis* their governments, those rights were based not on one's humanity *per se*, but on membership in the community, status or some other ascriptive characteristic.

Asmarom Legesse argues along similar lines that 'many studies have been carried out that suggest that distributive justice, in the economic and political spheres, is the cardinal ethical principle that is shared by most Africans' (1980:127). But distributive justice and human rights are quite different concepts. While a theory or conception of distributive justice might be based on human rights, it just as easily may be based on another principle. For example, Plato, Burke and Bentham had theories of distributive justice, yet no one would think to suggest that they advocated human rights.

Once again, many of the same things are valued, but the way in which they are valued — in particular the way these values are socially established and protected — is quite different. Recognition of human rights simply was not the way of traditional Africa. The available literature on traditional Asian perspectives is of much the same sort (see, e.g. Lo 1949; Leng 1980; Buultjens 1980).

None of this should be surprising; it is hardly novel to note the association of natural rights ideas and modern capitalism. Some of the implications of this will be addressed in Chapter 5. For now, it can simply be noted that traditional societies, wherever located, seem to have had no place for human rights.

To reduce the question to one of traditional versus modern would, however, be misleading; the concept and practice of human rights is no more uniquely modern than, say, totalitarianism. Human rights — universal rights/titles held equally by all simply because they are human beings — is one distinctive approach to securing human dignity. 'Human rights' refers to a particular social practice, not just any system of political right or an institutionally unspecified commitment to realise human dignity; it is one particular way in which the realisation of widely shared human values may be sought.

Human Rights and Utility

While it is generally agreed that utilitarianism represents an alternative to human rights, the great variety of utilitarian perspectives has made the exact nature of the utilitarian challenge rather ambiguous. Even Bentham's discussion of rights, utility and natural rights proceeds along a variety of tracks.

Bentham argues that rights are a 'fiction', i.e. an object 'which in every language must, for the purposes of discourse, be spoken of as existing' (1838:VIII, 198–9, 206, 247; 1970:251–2). As such, he is committed to presenting an exposition of the concept; a necessary fiction should be embedded in any ongoing system of political practices. Bentham's utilitarian account of rights, however, amounts to a repudiation of rights as ordinarily understood.

'Subservient to utility, there is no objection either to the word or the thing; that which is useful is *right*: a right is that which grows out of the application of the greatest happiness principle' (Bentham 1834:I, 136–7; compare 1838:II, 501, III, 159; 1970:58; 1952:I, 333). But the claim that a right is that which is useful confuses rights with what is right (as defined by utility) and thus is just a specification of the (inaccurate) simple-beneficiary theory discussed above. Furthermore, the *subservience of utility* to rights is the whole point of the special normative force of rights as trumps; subservient to utility, 'rights' are no longer rights.

Rights are not the record of utilitarian calculations — or rather, if they are it is a contingent fact of no conceptual significance. Utility does not determine which rights one has. Usually utility does not even determine which rights ought to be exercised, respected, enforced or overridden in particular cases. Ordinarily, rights simply are not subject to utilitarian validation of any sort.

Consider a case such as the nazi rally in the late seventies in Skokie, Illinois, a community with a sizable number of Jewish refugees and survivors of the Holocaust. Suppose that we are able to determine empirically, beyond all reasonable doubt, that letting the nazis march provides pleasure to a few and displeasure, even anguish, to a large number; i.e. that the balance of pleasure to pain unambiguously favours prohibiting the rally, even if we give full weight to the long-run costs of the precedents that might be established. None the less, if the rally is speech, as it seems to be, and if the Constitution guarantees the right to speak, as it clearly does, the rally must be permitted. This is simply the way entrenched basic rights work; a protection that did not work this way would not be a right.

Or suppose that virtually everyone in a society intensely enjoys torturing members of a fringe political group, so that a calculation of pleasures and pains establishes beyond all doubt that such torture would maximise utility. Such a determination would only increase the importance of rights to freedom of expression and personal liberty. The utility of torture does not imply that the intended victims have no rights, or even that their rights can be justifiably infringed.

Utilitarian calculations are not only irrelevant to whether or not one 'has' a right, but in most cases utility is not even the decisive factor in determining what ought to be done, all things considered. Suppose that A has an admitted surplus of money, to which he holds property rights, and B is destitute. Suppose further that a one-time transfer of money from A to B would increase the balance of pleasure, even considering the costs in terms of perceived security to A and others similarly situated. If utility (beneficial obligation) truly yielded rights, B would have a right to that money.[6] Central to the very idea of A's right to the money, however, is that B *doesn't* have a right to it (because A does, and the money is not a public good).

The existing distribution of funds in this example may be profoundly unjust. One way to establish this might be through a utilitarian calculation. None the less, A's right to the money largely insulates him from utilitarian claims; A's right, as it were, removes his money from the common fund from which all might be presumed to be justified in drawing on the basis of interest or need — and it is precisely such features of rights that cannot be captured in directly utilitarian terms.

Notice that I have yet to mention natural or human rights. This is because utilitarianism has nothing special to say about human rights, as opposed to other kinds of rights. Bentham's attacks on natural rights in particular, including his famous description of imprescriptible natural rights as 'nonsense upon stilts' (1838:II, 501), have absolutely nothing to do with utilitarianism. Instead, they rest on Bentham's legal positivism.

Bentham, at a number of points, argues — or rather, asserts — that 'there are no rights other than legal rights' (1838:III, 221, II, 500–1, VIII, 557; 1970:57, 63, 220, 291). This is simply an arbitrary stipulation. Furthermore, it is at odds not only with our ordinary understanding and practice, but with utilitarianism as well, since laws may easily conflict with utility, especially under Bentham's command theory of law. Either rights are 'the fruits of the law, and of the law alone' (1838:III, 221), or they are subservient to utility.

Utilitarianism is incompatible with natural or human rights not because they are *human* rights, but because they are rights. Rights simply do not work in the same way as considerations of utility; in numerous important cases, rights and utility prescribe different actions or evaluations.

None the less, the 'non-utilitarian' ways rights work may be capable of indirect utilitarian justification. Utilitarian moral theories usually are divided into two classes, act and rule utilitarianism. Act utilitarianism involves the direct application of the principle of utility to particular cases. Rule utilitarianism, however, applies the principle of utility directly (only) to 'rules' or social practices. Once a 'rule' has been justified as in sum consistent with utility, particular acts are judged by their conformity to the 'utilitarian' rule.

A rule-utilitarian theory of rights does seem to be possible in principle. However, it is largely without interest as a theory of rights because of its concentration on the compatibility of rights and utility. Even if we grant that rights and utility are compatible (in the sense that plausible utilitarian arguments can be advanced to 'justify' the practice in general as well as the implementation, respect or enforcement of numerous particular rights), a rule-utilitarian theory of rights tells us nothing about the nature, source or substance of rights. In fact, concentrating on the question of compatibility — which may be of some importance in evaluating utilitarianism as a general moral theory — is likely to obscure the fundamental differences between rights-based and utility-based moral and political theories and practices.

For example, a rule utilitarian may be able to justify the list of basic rights enumerated in, say, the French *Declaration of the Rights of Man and the Citizen*; i.e. such a set of rights might be shown to have social consequences which in sum are beneficial, making them (indirectly) 'utilitarian'. Such a utilitarian account, however, would seriously misrepresent the actual natural rights logic that Paine, for example, (correctly) argues underlies the *Declaration*. The actual justification of this set of rights stresses human *dignity*, the *human* person, rather than utility and largely undifferentiated interests and preferences. While a utilitarian may be able to provide some sort of after-the-fact 'justification' for a list of rights, it is difficult to imagine the list being generated from a utilitarian starting point.

Beginning with persons endowed with basic rights, whether by 'nature' or by the fundamental principles of a regime, we are likely to act and reason differently than if we begin with utility, as it were, *tabula rasa*. Rights-based theories rest on essentially qualitative moral judgements of persons and practices, as opposed to the fundamentally quantitative approach of utility.

Basic moral and political rights are not just weighting factors in utilitarian calculations that deal with an undifferentiated 'happiness'. Rather, they are demands and constraints of a different order, grounded in an essentially substantive judgement of the conditions necessary for human development and flourishing. They also provide means — rights — for realising human potentials. The neutrality of utilitarianism, its efforts to assure that everyone counts 'equally', results in no-one counting as a person; as Robert E. Goodin puts it, people drop out of utilitarian calculations, which are instead about disembodied preferences (1981:95; compare Dworkin 1977:94–100, 232–8, 274 ff.). In Aristotelian terms, utilitarianism errs in basing its judgements on 'numerical' rather than 'proportional' equality.

For our purposes, such differences should be highlighted. Therefore, let us consider utilitarianism, whether act or rule, as an alternative to rights in general, and thus human rights as well. In particular, we can consider utility and human rights as competing strategies for limiting the range of legitimate state action. Once again, Bentham provides a useful focus for our discussion.

While Bentham insists on the importance of limiting the range of legitimate state action (1838:II, 495, VIII, 557 ff.), he also insists that (natural) rights do not set those limits. In fact, he argues that construed as limits on the state, natural rights 'must ever be, — the rights of anarchy', justifying insurrection whenever a single right is violated (1838:II, 522, 496, 501, 506). For Bentham, natural rights are *absolute* rights, and thus inappropriate to the real world of political action.

In fact, though, no major human rights theorist argues that they are absolute. For example, Locke holds that the right to revolution is reserved by society, not the individual (1967: para. 243). Therefore, individual violations of human rights *per se* do not justify revolution. Furthermore, Locke supports revolution only in cases of gross, persistent and systematic violations of natural rights (1967: paras 204, 207, 225), as does Paine. The very idea of absolute rights is absurd from a human rights perspective, since logically there can be at most one absolute right, unless we (unreasonably) assume that rights never come into conflict.

A more modest claim would be that human rights are 'absolute' in the sense that they override all principles and practices except other human rights. Even this doctrine, however, is rejected by most if not all major human rights theorists and documents. For example,

Article 1 of the French *Declaration of the Rights of Man*, after declaring that 'men are born, and always continue, free and equal in respect of their rights', adds that 'civil distinctions, therefore, can be founded only on public utility', thus recognising restrictions on the continued complete equality of rights. Similarly, the *Universal Declaration of Human Rights* (Article 29) permits

> such limitations as are determined by law solely for the purpose of securing due recognition and respect for the rights and freedoms of others and of meeting the just requirements of morality, public order and the general welfare in a democratic society.

The *International Covenant on Civil and Political Rights* includes a similar general limiting proviso (Article 4) as well as particular limitations on most of the enumerated rights.

Rights ordinarily 'trump' other considerations, but the mere presence of a right — even a basic human right — does not absolutely and automatically determine the proper course of action, all things considered. In certain exceptional circumstances, needs, utility, interests or righteousness may override rights.

The duties correlative to rights, and even the trumping force of rights, are prima facie only. But other principles also have prima facie moral force. Sometimes this will be sufficient to overcome even the special entrenched priority of rights. The obligations arising from such rights therefore ought not to be discharged, all things considered. In such cases, we can speak of the right being 'infringed', since the (prima facie) obligation correlative to the right is not discharged, but it would be seriously misleading to say that it had been 'violated' (Thomson 1976, 1977).

But if even basic human rights can be justifiably infringed, aren't rights ultimately subservient to utility? If recalcitrant political realities sometimes require subordinating natural rights, aren't we simply suggesting that human rights are merely utopian aspirations inappropriate to a world in which dirty hands are often a requirement of political action — and thus where utility is the only reasonable guide?

Such a response misconstrues the relationship between rights and utility and the ways in which rights are overridden. Consider a very simple case, involving minor rights that on their face would seem to be easily overridden. If A promises to drive B and C to the movies but later changes his mind, in deciding whether to keep his promise (and discharge his rights-based obligations) A must consider more than the relative utilities of both courses of action for all the parties affected; in most cases, he ought to drive them to the movies even if that would reduce overall utility. At the very least he must ask them to excuse him from his obligation, this requirement (as well as the power to excuse) being a reflection of the right-holder's control over the rights relationship. Utility alone usually will not override even minor rights; we require more than a simple calculation of utility to justify infringing rights.

The special priority of rights/titles, as we have seen, implies that the quality, not just the quantity, of the countervailing forces (utilities) must be taken into consideration. For example, if, when the promised time comes, A wants instead to go get drunk with some other friends, simply not showing up to drive B and C to the movies will not be justifiable even if that would maximise utility; the desire for a drunken binge is not a consideration that ordinarily will justifiably override rights. But if A accompanies an accident victim to the hospital, even if A is only one of several passers-by who stopped to offer help, and his action proves to be of no real benefit to the victim, usually this will be a sufficient excuse, even if utility would be maximised by A going to the movies. Therefore, even recasting rights as weighted interests (which would seem to be the obvious utilitarian 'fix' to capture the special priority of rights) still misses the point, because it remains essentially quantitative.

Rights even tend to override an accumulation of comparable or parallel interests. Suppose that sacrificing a single innocent person with a rare blood factor could completely and permanently cure ten equally innocent victims of a disease that produces a sure, slow and agonising death. Each of the eleven has the 'same' right to life. Circumstances require, however, that a decision be made as to who will live and who will die. The natural rights theorist would almost certainly choose to protect the rights of the one individual — and such a conclusion, when faced with the scapegoat problem, is one of the greatest virtues of a natural rights doctrine to its advocates. This conclusion rests on a qualitative judgement that establishes the right, combined with the further judgement that it is not society's role to infringe such rights simply to foster utility, a judgement arising from the special moral priority of rights.

Politically, such considerations are clearest in the case of extremely unpopular minorities. For example, plausible arguments can be made that considerations of utility would justify persecution of selected religious minorities (e.g. Jews for centuries in the West, Mormons in nineteenth-century America, Jehovah's Witnesses in contemporary Malawi), even giving special weight to the interests of members of these minorities and considering the precedents set by such persecutions. None the less, human rights demand that an essentially qualitative judgement be made that such persecutions are incompatible with a truly human life and cannot be allowed — and such judgements go a long way to explaining the relative appeal of human rights theories.

But suppose that the sacrifice of one innocent person would save not ten but a thousand, or a hundred thousand, or a million people. All things considered, trading one innocent life for a million, even if the victim resists most forcefully, would seem to be not merely justifiable but demanded. Exactly how *do* we balance rights (in the sense of 'having a right'), wrongs (in the sense of 'what is right') and interests? Do the numbers count? If so, why, and in what way? If not, why not?

Ultimately the defender of human rights is forced back to human nature, the source of natural or human rights. For a natural rights theorist there are certain attributes, potentialities and holdings that are essential to the maintenance of a life worthy of a human being. These are given the special protection of natural rights; any 'utility' that might be served by their infringement or violation would be indefensible, literally inhuman — except in genuinely extraordinary circumstances, the possibility of which cannot be denied, but the probability of which should not be overestimated.

Extraordinary circumstances do force us to admit that, at some point, however rare, the force of utilitarian considerations builds up until quantity is transformed into quality. The human rights theorist, however, insists on the extreme rarity of such cases. Furthermore, exotic cases should not be permitted to obscure the fundamental difference in emphasis (and in the resulting judgements in virtually all cases) between utility and (human) rights. Nor should they be allowed to obscure the fact that on balance the flaws in rights-based theories and practices seem less severe, and without a doubt less numerous, than those of utility-based political strategies.

Another way to read utilitarianism would be as an objection to the priority human rights grant to the individual over society and the state. How can we justifiably require the state to protect the interests of the few, as expressed in rights, against the interests of the many or the whole, as determined by utilitarian calculation? On what grounds can we say that individuals are to be protected in certain special ways and, in their specially protected spheres, be given the liberty to exercise their rights so as to override virtually all other considerations — even, if necessary, stop the government dead in its tracks?

Natural rights theorists must again go back to 'human nature', in the special sense that term has in the constructivist theory. Inherent and inviolable human dignity, which it is the purpose of natural rights to protect, demands such special protection, even against society and the state (except in the most extreme circumstances). To do anything less would be to treat people as less than fully human. Thus the state is viewed as first an instrument to implement, protect and realise (human) rights; pursuit of the common good is an appropriate task for the government only in so far as it does not interfere with securing the enjoyment of human rights.

The 'equality' at the core of natural rights theories is a moral equality that rests on a substantive moral judgement of the type of life worthy of a human being. For the natural rights theorist all men 'are equal', but not all things which men share with one another are equally deserving of the protection of natural rights — particularly not their lower animal nature. The 'nature' that Bentham relies on is largely physical and 'quantitative', while the 'nature' underlying human rights is essentially moral.

Human rights represent the moral limits of state action established by 'human nature', understood constructively. Not only can one never be justly deprived of such rights, but even justifiable infringements are so severely restricted that for most purposes we can simply say that they set down what the state *cannot* do.

Bentham, however, takes special exception to precisely this claim.

> To denote legal impossibility . . . ['cannot' is] without ambiguity or inconvenience. 'Such a magistrate cannot do so and so,' that is, he has no power to do so and so. If he issue a command to such an effect, it is no more to be obeyed than if it issued from any private person. But when the same expression is applied to the very power which is acknowledged to be supreme, and not limited by any specific institution, clouds of ambiguity and confusion roll on in a torrent almost impossible to be withstood. (1838:II, 495)

If it is true that law can be limited only as to its source, not its substance, then it is nonsense to say that no law can be made which will do *x*. Such a conclusion, however, rests only on Bentham's peculiar definition of 'law' as the command of the sovereign. Besides this, Bentham has no real argument against a limited sovereign beyond his stipulation that the sovereign is above all other authority.

What truth there is to Bentham's argument lies in the familiar observation that, for example, should the French National Assembly desire to enact laws contrary to the *Declaration of the Rights of Man*, it could do so with ease — as in fact it later did. The willingness of the people to obey may be said to be the sole limit of what the government 'can' do, in the sense of what it can get away with. Natural rights advocates, however, are concerned with the quite different question of what the government can *legitimately* do; the legal and moral limits of state action, the sense of moral 'impossibility' against which Bentham explicitly argues.

Despite their moral basis, such limitations are not 'merely' moral; declarations of rights often have considerable practical importance. While parliament 'can' do anything it wishes to and can get away with, it is of far greater political significance that it 'cannot' do numerous things prohibited by custom and 'constitutional' rights. Likewise, in the United States the government 'cannot' do many things because it is prohibited from doing so by the *Bill of Rights*, not only in moral or legal theory, but as a matter of political fact.

This represents the partial realisation of the self-fulfilling prophecy of human rights; these political limits can be seen to be largely a function of the fact that the people in these countries will not permit their rights to be systematically infringed or violated, which in turn is largely a function of the fact that, as a result of the political practice of their countries, they have come to see these rights as essential to a life of dignity. Such limits on state action thus are the limits set by 'human nature', constructively understood.

Human rights limitations also have a variety of practical advantages over utility. They are far more clear, and more precise. Whatever the imprecision in 'the right to work', 'the right to vote', or 'the right to freedom of speech', such rights provide more concrete guidance than 'utility'. Furthermore, a full set of rights provides a range of restraints that in practice is almost certain to be far more precise; the counterpart to the 'simplicity' of utility as a single standard for evaluating all conduct is the vagueness of a single, universally applicable standard. This provides far greater predictability for both right-holders and duty-bearers. To draw a legal analogy, rights function more like laws that have been promulgated, whereas utility, especially act utilitarianism, works more like unelaborated expressions of the desire of the sovereign. Rights publicly announce, with *relatively* little ambiguity, the limits of state action, thus simplifying the life of citizens and government officials alike.

Furthermore, rights held against the government establish conditions for a particularly active citizen, and this active participation is highly valued. Merely utilitarian restraints are quite compatible with being a passive subject. When applied to the foundations and regulation of the state, utility, like natural law — and, as we shall see, like prescription as well — has a strong tendency towards paternalism. Rights carve out a specially protected sphere of individual freedom that is largely under the control of the right-holder.[7] Fostering the development of such autonomous individuals lies at the heart of the human rights approach and of most particular human rights. So long as the resulting individualism is not 'excessive' or atomising — a problem discussed in Chapter 5 — this would seem to be one of the greatest advantages of the human rights approach.

Reason, History and Political Restraint

Still another alternative to human rights is presented by prescription, the view that a people's past usage and customs provide authoritative political guidelines, including an authoritative distribution of political rights and duties. This strategy for restraining the state, associated particularly with Burke, differs fundamentally from the others we have considered so far. Rather than rely on 'external' checks, such as utility or natural law, Burke attempts to integrate the ruler into a constraining web of prescriptive practices. Thus, like human rights institutionalised as constitutional rights, Burke builds limitations on the state into its very structure. But where human rights shares with natural law and utility a fundamental reliance on reason, Burke rejects reason in favour of history.

Burke argues that sovereign and subjects are coordinate parts of the state, and thus neither may legitimately alter the form of government or the distribution of rights and duties (1869:III, 257–8; IV, 161–2). The organic conception of the state and society that this implies will be addressed, in a rather different context, in Chapter 5. Here I want to stress the essential historicism of Burke's theory.

Natural rights theorists view the government as possessed of duties to the people, not rights (other than a right to remuneration for services rendered) (see, e.g. Paine 1945:I, 379; Priestley 1791:29; Rous 1791a:67–8). The ruler, for Burke, however, is not an employee removable at the discretion of the people, but a contracting party, with rights as well as obligations, including a right to rule. This right, Burke argues, cannot be revoked for anything short of malfeasance of the very grossest sort (1869:III, 266 ff.; IV, 161–2, 429).

None the less, the sovereign is restricted in what he may legitimately do. Although he is, as sovereign, literally neither responsible nor accountable to anyone (1869:III, 267), his power is not unlimited or arbitrary; like all power, it remains under the guidance of justice, morality and right reason and must be guided by considerations of prudence and what is right — but not abstract and general rights (1869:III, 257). The most important limit on the sovereign's power, however, is prescription.

For Burke, all political titles rest on prescription, the established usages of a people. 'All titles terminate in prescription' (1869:VI, 412), including, and most particularly, the title to rule.

> Our Constitution is a prescriptive constitution; it is a constitution whose sole authority is, that it has existed time out of mind . . . Prescription is the most solid of all titles, not only to property, but, which is to secure that property, to government. (1869:VI, 94)

Society and government — and of course rights as well — are, for Burke, historical products; they are not created by plan, but evolve in response to social wants and needs as they emerge in the historical experience of a people. Therefore, established institutions and practices represent the record of successful incremental adjustments, compromises and reforms, and thus deserve special respect and protection.

Prescriptive title, for Burke, is 'a deliberate election of ages and generations' (1869:VI, 95), an expression of the ongoing intergenerational social contract (1869:III, 359), and a prima facie demonstration of a practice's social utility. Furthermore, the prescriptive practice is not only well tested, but integrated into an ongoing, functioning set of practices in harmony with the circumstances and experience of a nation. While such practices may appear 'irrational' to a detached observer newly on the scene, they are eminently functional, as attested by long experience; they may not be maximally efficient or Pareto optimal, but they do 'get the job done'.

The fact that prescriptive practices have proved themselves adequate to the task is particularly important when it comes to choosing between competing policies and institutions, since radical reforms risk abandoning a present good for a perhaps unattainable or even illusory future gain. Furthermore, because of the intricate structure and interconnections of human institutions, major reforms are likely to have wide-ranging unintended consequences, as changes work their way through the delicately articulated parts of a society and government. Since a large and indeterminate range of practices may be threatened by any substantial reform, it becomes particularly difficult to make the rational assessment of costs and benefits needed to justify major reforms or revolution. For Burke, the choice is between order and natural rights, and, as we saw above, he presents the French Revolution as an example of what can be expected if natural rights are put into practice.

Burke, however, largely overlooks the costs of prescription, which are at least as high. The substance of the rights of citizens in a prescriptive regime is historically contingent, almost accidental. Prescription is a procedural principle of justice and therefore rests on the relative certainty that the procedure — history — will produce beneficial results. We know, though, that besides justice or utility, power, force, ignorance or subtle forms of coercion may produce popular acquiescence, even over decades; the beneficiaries of prescriptive practices may be only a small elite. Therefore, prescription is at best only a prima facie test of justice or utility; an additional substantive test is required. For this Burke turns to natural law.

For example, he suggests that the enormity of the moral offences of the French Revolution make it hard to imagine it ever being sanctified by prescription (1869:III, 451). Furthermore, when prescription is not available Burke draws freely on arguments of natural law and natural justice, most notably in his speeches during the impeachment and trial of Warren Hastings, the former Governor-General of India, whom Burke accuses of violating 'those eternal laws of justice which are our rule and birthright', the principles of 'natural, immutable and substantial justice' (1869:IX, 338, 340; compare IX, 445–63).

Burke argues that 'the laws of morality are the same everywhere' (1869:IX, 448). He even speaks of 'the principles of natural equity, and of the Law of Nations, which is the birthright of us all' (1869:XI, 241). And this law is not only our birthright, it is 'indefeasible' (1869:IX, 459) and underlies all valid human institutions. 'This great law does not arise from our conventions or compacts; on the contrary, it gives to our conventions and compacts all the force and sanction they can have' (1869:IX, 455–6). Thus there are certain practices that simply could never be valid for Burke, that could never achieve the sanction of prescription.

However, once Burke allows that prescription is limited by natural law, government is opened to the claims of reason, substantive justice and natural rights. Once prescription is recognised to have its limits, the problem, from a Burkean perspective, is to keep those limits restricted in number and extent, and to keep them from evolving into general, 'abstract' arguments of reason and universal rights. Burke, however, never manages to resolve, or even seriously to pursue, this tension between concrete procedural principles and more speculative substantive principles; he appears as both a proto-historicist, arguing for a nearly unrestricted doctrine of prescription and the primacy of prudence and convention in politics, and a natural law theorist, vigorously opposed to an extreme or excessive historical relativism.

Any theory must face the problem of reconciling the obvious political importance of prudence and convention with the equally important demands of substantive principles of justice and morality; to choose only one side is to lapse into either an amoral relativism or an abstract idealism. One of the great attractions of a constructivist theory of human rights is the fruitful merging of the universal and the particular. In contrast, the two sides appear in Burke's work, but are not successfully fused.

Burke's historicism, however, does provide an illuminating counterpoint to *all* the other approaches we have considered here. Thomistic natural law, Lockean natural rights and Benthamite utilitarianism all rely primarily on reason in constructing and controlling the state. For Locke, the most optimistic and rationalistic of the three (despite his empiricism and eudaemonism), natural law/reason, if only it is consulted, can prevent the passions from misleading us into corruption, unhappiness and discord; even the state of nature is not necessarily a state of war, and Locke suggests that it is at least relatively easy for man in society to cultivate his reason and conform his actions to the natural law. Paine presents much the same argument implicitly, while Benthamite social engineering has a similar, essentially rationalistic basis.

Aquinas is more a frustrated rationalist. Although he has much the same idea of the restraining function of reason, Aquinas sees reason alone as insufficient to the task. Reason tells man what he should do, but man's will is too weak, too corrupted by pride and passion to follow this guidance without the additional backing of coercion by the state. Thus Aquinas, much like Hobbes, vacillates between reason and power in his political thought.

'Reason', however, has an entirely different nature in Burke's theory. The speculative reason of Aquinas, Hobbes, Locke and Bentham is excluded from politics and replaced by a reason that is 'practical' in the most concrete sense. Political reason — prudence, operating within the confines of tradition — is Burke's guide, and it is, as Burke calls justice itself, 'a circumspect, cautious, scrutinizing, balancing principle' (1869:XI, 181), rather than an abstract and general guide.

In the realm of rights this stress on the particular appears in many forms. For example, Burke, when speaking favourably of natural rights, tends to speak of the rights of men, in the plural (1869:II, 437, III, 308, IX, 463) rather than the rights of man; i.e. of the concrete rights of particular individuals rather than of human beings in general. Similarly, Burke prefers arguments based on civil rights, or at most what he calls 'the *chartered rights of man*' (1869:II, 437); i.e. not original natural rights *per se* (even assuming that they exist), but those rights as they have been backed and transformed by the sovereign power and sanctified in the great charters. These rights have the sanction of reason — but concrete reason based on history, experience and prescription.

Like Aquinas, Hobbes and Locke, Burke's reason does seek after the common good and the good of mankind — but through the experiential wisdom of traditional practices rather than abstract principles. As a result, both the sovereign and the popular passions are held in check by a single principle, prescription. This binding is much more concrete and pressing than the bonds of a natural law unsupported by natural rights, while avoiding the risks of anarchy and insufficient restraint that Burke sees as inherent in a natural rights doctrine. History, in the form of prescription, thus combines the functions of reason, utility, power, natural law and natural rights.

The weight of historical experience, however, suggests that such a system of restraints is impractical. As with Bentham, Burke's average citizen is a beneficiary of government's activity but not the master of the government. Thus those whose interests are at stake — particularly the mass of the people, who are most in need of protection from the state — are not empowered to look after and protect their own interests. The approach is essentially paternalistic. This renders it largely unsuited to the real world of human frailties. Ironically, while prescriptive restraint has a certain abstract, theoretical plausibility, in practice it would seem to require an ideal world ruled by true natural aristocrats, uncorrupted by the seductions of power and self-interest.

For example, Burke's theory of virtual representation (see Pitkin 1967:168–89 and 237–9) may have its attractions and justifications *if* the representatives measure up to the Burkean ideal. However, historical experience, for example, with the English rotten boroughs or American racial gerrymandering, clearly suggests that this assumption will only rarely hold true. The natural rights alternative of popular sovereignty at least provides a certain amount of power to the people over their representatives, which is a distinctly *practical* advantage, despite its 'abstract' rational basis in a theory of human rights.

Similar problems beset Burke's claim that 'all men have equal rights' in society.

> Whatever each man can separately do, without trespassing upon others, he has a right to do for himself; and he has a right to a fair portion of all which society, with all its combinations of skill and force, can do in his favor. In this partnership [society] all men have equal rights; but not to equal things. He that has but five shillings in the partnership has as good a right to it as he that has five hundred pounds has to his larger portion; but he has not a

right to an equal division in the product of the joint stock. (1869:III, 309)

By 'equal' Burke has in mind something like the sense in the claim 'I have as much a right to my five shillings as you do to your five hundred pounds'. Such 'equality' involves the equal protection of rights, whatever their substance; i.e. treating large and small alike without preference.

But while this is true and important, there are equally important senses in which these rights are grossly 'unequal'. As Burke himself notes, they are to 'unequal things'; i.e. the shares are unequal. Furthermore, if participation in the decisions of the partnership is on the basis of shares held, the rights are unequal in terms of the control they give over the actions of that partnership. When the partnership is society and the control is control over the government, the inequality is certain to seem to predominate, while the equality is likely to seem largely formal if not illusory.

While Burke recognises the right of each member of society to have his interests considered in political decisions, only those with substantial property or education have a right to participate in the political process directly. It is precisely this participation and control that (human) rights provide; in a regime based on the rights of man, citizens are sovereign rather than subjects or mere beneficiaries, as they are in regimes based on natural law, utility or prescription.

Burke's stress on history, experience and the particular provides a salutary reminder of the dangers of abstract speculation in political matters, and of the risks, and difficulties, of radical change and social engineering, whether based on rights, utility or some other principle. A constructivist theory, however, seems able to incorporate these important insights while overcoming all of Burke's major theoretical and practical objections. Natural rights limits on state action are reasonable and, as the experience of several contemporary liberal democratic regimes suggests, quite practical; the constitutional entrenchment of basic rights can provide protections that meet the demands of human rights at an acceptable political cost.

Notes

1. There is no incompatibility between the idea of human rights setting the limits of state action and the fact that human rights are claimed primarily when unenforceable — so long as we distinguish having and claiming a right. Widely effective human rights restraints on the state usually will take the form of entrenched constitutional rights (or some analogous practice such as common law rights); this is implied by rights-claims aiming to be self-liquidating. In a regime governed according to such principles, citizens will not *claim* human rights, but the legal rights they do claim will have a fundamental human rights basis. Therefore, we can properly speak of human rights restraints even in such cases. This is underscored by the fact that if these 'lower' rights do not suffice, people will claim the human rights they have had (but not used) all along.

2. In this section all otherwise unidentified references (marked with square brackets for clarity) are to Aquinas' *Summa Theologica* — i.e. Aquinas 1913 — by Part, Question, Article and, where appropriate, Reply. For example, 1a2ae, 90.1 ad 1 would indicate first part (1a) of the second part (2ae), question 90 (90), article 1 (.1), reply to the first objection (ad 1). All citations unidentified by part are to 1a2ae, 90–7 (the first eight questions of 'The Treatise on Law'). Thus this particular passage is from the first part of the second part of the *Summa*, question 90, article 4.

3. These conditions are slightly different from those in the definition of law. Accord with reason and promulgation are left implicit, promulgation being obviously necessary for one to be aware of one's obligation, and reason being either implied by the common good or so obvious as not to require mention. The one new factor, proportionality, is a requirement of justice, a topic which is treated most fully at 2a2ae, 58 and 60.

4. Furthermore, Aquinas explicitly views tyranny as a divine scourge visited upon sinful peoples (1949: para. 51) and notes that 'As the Apostle says, all human power is from God' [96.4 ad 1]. Compare 93.3 ad 2 and *Summa Contra Gentes* II, 81.

5. See, for example, Mawdudi 1976:10; Nadvi 1966:14–15; Tabandeh 1970:1, 85; Ishaque 1974:32–8; Said 1979:65–8; Khadduri 1946:77–8; Hassan 1982:55 ff.

6. This case suggests the difficulty of constructing a system and functioning practice of rights along utilitarian lines. 'Having' a right to x at time t would, under such a theory, be no guarantee that, despite doing nothing to alienate the right, one may end up not having it at time u.

7. This should not be taken to imply that human rights are merely 'negative' rights (i.e. rights that require only the forbearance of duty-bearers). This sphere of freedom may be defined to include 'positive' rights as well; for example, rights to work, education and health care that might be viewed as necessary for the true enjoyment of even negative liberties. The issue of positive versus negative rights is addressed in some detail in Chapter 6.

5 INDIVIDUALISM AND HUMAN RIGHTS: FURTHER CHALLENGES TO HUMAN RIGHTS

We have already touched on the charge that rights-based theories and institutions engender excessive individualism. In this chapter we will consider in more detail three versions of such an argument: (1) the Strauss-Macpherson thesis that Lockean liberalism, which lies at the heart of the natural rights tradition, rests on the sanctification of (bourgeois) self-interest; (2) Marxist arguments against the individualism of human rights, both as developed by Marx himself and as they appear in contemporary Soviet theory and practice; and (3) arguments from the Third World for less individualistic conceptions of human rights.

Egoism and the Foundations of Natural Rights

In discussing Locke, Leo Strauss, with characteristic exaggeration, claims that 'through the shift in emphasis from natural duties or obligations to natural rights, the individual, the ego, has become the center and origin of the moral world' (1953:248). In fact, for Locke, God is the source of natural law, which is a law of reason not individual interests, and natural law obliges both in the state of nature and in society (Locke 1967: paras 6, 12, 16, 57, 59, 60, 118, 124, 135, 172; 1954:214; 1975:I, sect. 1.5, 4.2, II, sect. 9.12, 23.12). In other words, the ego is not the *origin* of Locke's moral world. The less extreme view that natural rights rest on a corrosive individualism does, however, present a more serious challenge to human rights. Strauss and C.B. Macpherson have developed such arguments with particular reference to the foundations of Anglo-American liberalism, the historical source of natural rights theories.

Strauss characterises Locke's theory of natural rights as little more than a rationalisation and glorification of a base natural desire for self-preservation (1953:226 ff., 234 ff.).

> The desire for happiness and the pursuit of happiness have [for Locke] the character of an absolute right, of a natural

right . . . Since happiness presupposes life, the desire for life takes precedence over the desire for happiness in case of conflict . . . The most fundamental of all rights is therefore the right of self-preservation. (1953:226–7)

Strauss continues by arguing that for Locke natural law amounts to little more than the dictates of instrumental reason aimed at assuring peace and security so as to protect one's life (1953:228–9).

Locke does write of the 'Fundamental, Sacred and unalterable Law of *Self-Preservation*'; he even argues that everyone is 'bound to preserve himself' (1967: paras 149, 9). However, Locke also writes that *'the first and fundamental natural Law . . .* is *the preservation of Society.'* 'Nature . . . willeth the preservation of all Mankind as much as is possible' (1967: paras 134, 182, 16, 135, 159). Such passages suggest quite a different first principle, 'the Peace and *preservation of all Mankind*' (1967: para. 7), which we can call the principle of 'species-preservation'.

For Locke, *each* man has a right — and duty (1967: para. 23) — to preserve himself. This severely limits the range of actions legitimately available to any one person in pursuit of his own self-preservation. In fact, Locke goes so far as to argue that the right to life may be forfeited by threatening the lives of others (1967: paras 16, 183); it is by no means an absolute right. Furthermore, the natural law injunction to species-preservation is not cancelled, even if it may be limited, by the right to self-preservation. And in no case will either self-preservation or species-preservation justify killing another: man 'has not Liberty to destroy himself or so much as any Creature in his possession, but where some nobler use, than its bare Preservation, calls for it' (1967: para. 6).

Therefore, in sharp contrast to Strauss's interpretation, Locke concludes that in cases where some life must be lost, preference is to be given to preservation of the innocent (not oneself): 'For *by the Fundamental Law of Nature, Man being to be preserved*, as much as possible, when all cannot be preserv'd, the safety of the Innocent is to be preferred' (1967: para. 16). The right to self-preservation thus is exactly a right to self-preservation or self-defence, narrowly understood as protection of oneself from destructive attack. Locke even indicates that the injunctions of self-preservation and species preservation have a single source — 'as he is *bound to preserve himself* . . . so by like reason . . . ought he, as much as he can, *to preserve the rest of Mankind*' (1967: para. 6) — and in his summation of man's liberty in the state of nature, he treats self-preservation and species-preservation as a single right (1967: para. 128).[1]

In fact, it would be inaccurate to suggest that mere preservation of *any* sort is the essential aim of natural law, natural rights, society or the state for Locke. Natural law aims to make man more rational and a better, more moral, creature (1967: paras 4, 6, 11–14, 57, 195; 1975:II, sect. 21.7–12, 47, 52, 53, 67). Both self-preservation and species-preservation are necessary for such improvement, but they are by no means sufficient to discharge the obligations of the natural law; the *way* in which life is protected, and the quality of that life, also are essential. Protecting the lives of the citizenry will not legitimise a government that systematically infringes other natural rights and transgresses the natural law (1967: paras 31, 135–7, 155, 168, 208, 220, 225, 235, 240, 243). Self-preservation — that is, the right to life — is of undeniable importance to Locke, but it is not the sole centre of Locke's moral world, nor does it override other natural rights or the natural law.

Rather than mere preservation, Macpherson, taking off from Locke's extensive discussion of the right to property, argues that acquisition — 'possessive individualism' — is the basis of Locke's theory of natural rights. Macpherson (1963:263–4) argues that Locke, and liberalism in general, view 'humanity' as freedom from dependence on the wills of others, see the individual as the sole and autonomous proprietor of his own person and capacities (including, and especially, the right to alienate this 'property'), present society as a series of market relationships, and conceive of political society as a contrivance to regulate these relationships so as to protect an individual's property in his person and goods. Despite the equality in natural rights in the state of nature and an apparent maintenance of equal rights in society, Macpherson argues that Locke, through his account of property, transforms natural rights into a device to justify and maintain differential, class-based, economic and political rights (1963: Chap. IV).

The heart of the interpretative problem lies in Locke's use of 'property' in three major senses: (1) possessions or 'estates' only (1967: paras 31, 32, 136, 139, 222); (2) 'Lives, Liberties and Estates, which I call by the general Name Property' (1967: paras 85, 87, 123); and (3) as a synonym for right in the sense of 'having a right'.

This third, and least noted sense is most clear when he speaks of a property in or to something. For example, Locke writes that 'every man has a *Property* in his own *Person*. This no body has a Right to but himself' (1967: paras 27, 190, 194). When he writes that a man 'hath *begun a Property*' when he has expended labour on the common stock of nature (1967: para. 30), the sense intended is equally rendered by 'has established a right'. At other points (e.g. paras 190, 194) Locke conveys the same idea by talking of rights in one's person.

Such usage would be odd today, at least in the United States, but it is well established. It is also quite 'natural', once we conceive of rights as titles, given the close connection between 'title' and 'property', both in Locke (1967: paras 32, 34, 39, 51) and in our own usage. Property rights, narrowly conceived as estates only, give special prominence to such essential aspects of the practice of rights as title, claims and control. Furthermore, property has been, historically, one of the most important things to which people have been held to possess legal and moral rights. While this does not give any special theoretical priority to property (estates) in discussions of lists of rights, it does help to explain, in much more neutral terms, Locke's occasional equation of 'rights' and 'property'.

Government, according to Locke, is obliged to preserve the property of its citizens (1967: paras 127, 138–40). If by this he means possessions alone, there does indeed seem to be a sinister element in the theory. However, if he means either life, liberty and estates, or rights in general — i.e. either the second or third sense of 'property' — things are quite different and, for our purposes, particularly interesting. Furthermore, even if Locke did occasionally lapse into taking this to mean estates only, later natural rights theorists are under no obligation to repeat his error — and it is an error, not only in substance but also in the context of Locke's broader theory, since he does seem committed to one (or both) of the latter senses of 'property'.

While life, liberty and possessions hardly exhaust the range of objects to which people have natural rights — and thus Locke can be argued to have had a limited conception of the substance of human rights — they are a far cry from possessive, atomistic individualism, particularly if 'liberty' is given a fairly broad interpretation. Thus Macpherson is incorrect to suggest that protection of possessions largely exhausts the rights-based obligations of Locke's government to its subjects. Citizens *have a right* to have the full range of natural rights respected. Failure to discharge this obligation authorises the people to act to dissolve the government.[2]

Locke's theory is essentially individualistic, and this is a consequence of the transformation of natural law into natural rights/entitlements, with all that implies. This 'individualism' may be subject to abuse. In its defence, however, I would suggest that the most likely sorts of abuses seem to be far less dangerous, for both the individual and society, than the abuse of power by a sovereign constrained by natural law alone, or some other non-rights mechanism. In the remainder of this chapter I will try to develop this suggestion more fully.

Marxism and Human Rights

Like any issue of Marxist theory, the question of the Marxist conception of human rights is wildly contentious (compare Lukes 1982b; Markovic 1982 and Macfarlane 1982). Certainly this is not the place to try to resolve the theoretical and ideological issues in such disputes. Marx's own views on human rights, and contemporary Soviet theory and practice, however, do raise issues of a more general nature connected with the question of individualism.

Marx's most extended discussion of the rights of man is in 'On the Jewish Question', where he presents a scathing indictment of natural rights ideas as the ideological expression of bourgeois egoism and social atomisation.

> the so-called *rights of man* . . . are nothing but . . . the rights of egoistic man, of man separated from other men and from the community. (1975:III, 162)
>
> None of the so-called rights of man, therefore, go beyond egoistic man, beyond man as a member of civil society, that is, an individual withdrawn into himself, and separated from the community. (1975:III, 164)

In summarising this argument in *The Holy Family*, Marx and Engels particularly emphasise the necessary connection between bourgeois society and human rights ideas.

> The *recognition of the rights of man* by the *modern state* has no
> other meaning than the *recognition of slavery* by the *state of
> antiquity* did. In other words, just as the ancient state had slavery
> as its *natural basis*, the *modern state* has as its *natural basis* civil
> society and the *man* of civil society, i.e. the individual man linked
> with other men only by the ties of private interest and *uncon-
> scious* natural necessity, the *slave* of labor for gain and of his own
> as well as other men's *selfish* needs. The modern state has
> recognized this its natural basis as such in the *universal rights of
> man*. It did not create it. As it was the product of civil society
> driven beyond the old political bounds by its own development,
> the modern state, for its part, now recognized the womb from
> which it sprang and its basis by the *declaration* of the *rights of
> man*. (1975:IV, 113)

There can be no doubt that Marx saw the rights of man, like
capitalism to which they were linked, as having played a positive, if
limited, historical role that was coming to an end; i.e. human rights
were seen by Marx as obsolescent and to be transcended in
socialism. But what would such transcendence look like? To resort
to Hegelian jargon, in the dialectical leap to socialism the lower
elements are both cancelled and preserved. Which elements of
'bourgeois' natural rights are to be 'cancelled' and which 'preserved'? Clearly socialist society will look very different if human
rights are primarily cancelled than if they are primarily preserved in
the transcendence. The central interpretative question, therefore, is
whether bourgeois (natural) rights are to be supplemented or sup-
planted in socialism.

Marx clearly objects to the *substance* of the bourgeois rights of
man, particularly as they were implemented by the bourgeois state.
If this were the whole of his argument, the remedy would be a
change in the list of human rights, adding some, dropping others
(especially the right to private property) and reinterpreting still
others in light of new social purposes and newly established rights;
in other words, bourgeois rights would be primarily supplemented.
Another side of Marx's argument, however, suggests a more
thoroughgoing objection to rights.

In the *Critique of the Gotha Program* Marx explicitly addresses
the question of rights in socialism with respect to the worker's com-
pensation for labour. In the early stages of socialism, a phase 'still

stamped with the birth marks of the old society from whose womb it emerges', the worker would contribute a quantity of labour and thus acquire a right to receive back a share of the social product (less necessary deductions) exactly proportional to his contribution. Marx criticises such an arrangement in terms that suggest opposition to the fundamental character of the practice of rights.

> A given amount of labor in one form is exchanged for an equal amount of labor in another form. Hence, *equal right* here is still in principle — *bourgeois right* . . . the equality consists in the fact that measurement is made with an *equal standard*, labor. *It is, therefore, a right of inequality, in its content, like every right.* Right by its very nature can consist only in the application of an equal standard; but unequal individuals (and they would not be different individuals if they were not unequal) are measurable only by an equal standard in so far as they are brought under an equal point of view, are taken from one *definite* side only, . . . everything else being ignored. (1968:324)

Only at a higher phase, when subordination to the division of labour has been overcome, 'only then can the narrow horizon of bourgeois right be crossed in its entirety and society inscribe on its banners: From each according to his ability, to each according to his needs!' (1968:325; compare Weil 1973:9–23).

Rights select particular aspects of a person's existence for special protection. As a result, Marx argues, the person as a whole is subordinated to particular parts of his personality. This abstraction is then intensified by the general form of rights, which does further violence to the uniqueness of real persons. Clearly, human rights are particularly subject to such criticisms, and they introduce a further 'abstraction' by their primarily political focus.

The abstract individualism of rights runs even deeper than this, however, because Marx sees right-holders as individuals set in opposition to other individuals, groups, and the community as a whole; he sees all rights as essentially rights *against* other persons and institutions, making human rights, which are held against all other persons, groups and institutions, particularly objectionable. The very notion of rights, according to Marx, is tied to the competitive struggle that characterises class societies (and bourgeois society in particular), and rests on a vision of society and the individual as inherently separate and antagonistic units. Rights, for Marx, are essentially instruments for carrying out adversary relations between competing, essentially atomistic, individuals.

It cannot be denied that there is an adversarial element in many rights relationships, especially those that involve assertive or remedial exercises. This is only one side of the practice, though. Equally important is the co-operation between right-holders and duty-bearers, especially in the standard cases of objective and direct enjoyment; in fact, these co-operative aspects of the practice are essential to its maintenance, as we saw above. I would argue, then, that rights represent a reasonable compromise between competition and co-operation, as well as an effective way to balance the unavoidable conflicts of interest between different individuals and between individuals and society — particularly in light of the alternatives.

So long as there is a state, it is almost certain to be used to further the interests of those who control it. Given the enormous reach and power of the modern state, such a threat to human dignity cannot be safely ignored; some sort of institutional mechanism of restraint is required. I have already argued that human rights provide a relatively well-developed and at least potentially effective restraint. Therefore, if they are to be abandoned, they must be replaced by an alternative mechanism or the threat posed by the state must be eliminated. Marx opts for this latter course.

As is well known, Marx argues that the state will atrophy once classes are eliminated. Therefore, proletarian socialist revolution, by eliminating the state, would remove the need for human rights. If conflict between individuals is also essentially class based, most other sorts of rights would also become unnecessary. Until these conditions are satisfied, however, rights will be abandoned only at great cost to human dignity. Once man and society have reached the higher phase of communism, rights may become a superfluous anachronism, but until then, they would seem to be necessary — on Marx's own argument.

Marx criticises the bourgeois character of rights in the early, transitional phase of socialism, from the point of view of the coming higher phase; but as we saw, he does not call for abandoning them *at this point* (1968:324–35). Likewise, 'bourgeois' human rights in bourgeois democratic republics are criticised for being partial, but Marx does not suggest that they simply be abolished, for their abolition would mark a return to an even lower stage of despotism. The early stages of socialism can even be seen as a consistent, impartial and universal extension of the principles of bourgeois right.

Whatever their shortcomings, when viewed in terms of future socialist principles, the rights characteristic of liberal democratic regimes are, from Marx's own point of view, undeniably superior to all other previously realised systems of rights and privileges. Some higher standard of human development may ultimately allow us to transcend human rights. Today, however, and for at least many decades to come, the pressing problem in virtually all countries is to ascend to the level where basic human rights are respected and enforced and the human possibilities that are their basis are realised. Until the revolution — the final revolution in which classes and the state are abolished and the tyranny of the division of labour overcome — human rights, from a Marxist perspective, have an important, if ultimately limited role in the struggle for human emancipation and dignity.

As I see the prospects of such a revolution as faint at best, I stress human rights as a political solution to the modern problems of human dignity; rather than emphasise Marxian revolutionary action to remove the need for human rights, I stress the implementation and further development of human rights. I might also add that given existing political conditions in most of the world, even this would be, in its own way, profoundly revolutionary.

This reading of Marx, however, is quite different from that provided by contemporary Soviet theory and practice. As with Marx himself, there are two strands to the Soviet critique of 'Western' human rights: an argument against the Western emphasis on civil and political rights, and a more fundamental uneasiness with the very nature of the practice. In light of the wide range of economic and social rights recognised and implemented in most Western countries (including even 'conservative' states such as the United States), the latter objection is the only one that any longer merits serious consideration.

The Soviet argument focuses on the relationship between rights and duties. The Preamble of the 1977 Constitution states that the USSR 'is a society of genuine democracy, whose political system ensures . . . the combination of real citizen's rights and liberties with their duties and responsibilities to society.' Article 59 states that 'the exercise of rights and liberties is inseparable from the performance by citizens of their duties.' Semi-official accounts present the matter in much the same way: 'the linkage of rights and duties [is] the special quality of socialist law' (Sawczuk 1979:89); 'the most important feature of the Soviet citizen's legal status is the organic unity between their rights and their obligations' (Chkhidvadze 1980:18). We can view this as one (very extreme) strategy for checking the inherent individualism of rights — making rights contingent on the performance of social duties.

As we have seen, A's right to x implies certain duties of B to A with respect to A's enjoyment of x (see also Donnelly 1982a). Soviet doctrine, however, not only reverses the standard direction of the correlation of rights and duties, incorrectly deriving rights from duties, but it also changes the duty-bearer, viewing A's right as entailing substantively parallel obligations *on the part of A*.

For example, Article 40 of the Soviet Constitution states that 'USSR citizens have the right to labour . . . including the right to choice of occupation, type of employment and work.' However, in Article 60 labour is presented as a citizen's duty: 'Conscientious labour in one's chosen field of socially useful activity and the observance of labour discipline are the duty of, and a matter of honour for, every able-bodied USSR citizen.' Soviet diplomats have been quite open in admitting that 'it [is] considered the individual's duty, as well as his right, to work for the benefit of society.'[3] How, though, can rights and duties be conceptualised as coincident?

It is sometimes suggested, not only by the Soviets, that this is just the way rights are, that the conceptual logic of rights entails that A's rights imply duties for A.

> Rights and duties are two facets of the same picture. Whoever demands a right to liberty has to respect a similar right in others which circumscribes his right to personal liberty very considerably. If an individual thinks it his right to be fed and clothed and maintained in proper health and if he has a right to work, it is also his duty to work according to his energies and skill and accept the work which the welfare of the community demands from him. (Hakim 1955:3)[4]

In fact, though, these duties, which we certainly do recognise, are not ordinarily viewed as arising from the possession of rights; or rather, not from one's own rights.

For example, the duty to respect another person's liberty is imposed on me by his right to liberty, not mine, and he has such a right not because I have a right to liberty but as a result of a particular (natural or social) pattern of the distribution of rights. Likewise, I can have a right to work or to health care without being under an obligation to work for, or contribute to, the welfare of the community; it may be an unjust or immoral society that gives me such rights without these duties, but there is no conceptual reason why it can't.

If the logic of rights does not render rights and duties coincident, the only way I can see to do so is to treat rights as social grants. If a society gives jobs to its citizens on condition that they accept parallel duties to work, the right to work would become simultaneously a duty, as a result of this mutually beneficial 'contract'.

This interpretation captures the Soviet emphasis on the social, rather than the individual. It also emphasises objective and concrete, rather than abstract or universal, rights, again in line with the basic philosophical and ideological precepts of the Soviet system. Such rights, however, are not *human* rights; they are simply (conditional) grants of society. Furthermore, they result in a subordination of the individual to society that is even more objectionable than the allegedly excessive individualism of human rights.

'The significance and worth of each person are determined by the way he exercises his rights and performs his duties' (Egorov 1979:36). At issue here is a conceptual point, not merely a dispute over the contents of a list of rights. Not only are civil and political rights granted solely 'in accordance with the people's interests and for the purpose of strengthening and developing the socialist system' (Article 50), but economic and social rights are equally contingent. For example, jobs in one's field are regularly denied to dissidents and to Jews seeking emigration, and émigrés may be legally required to buy back the 'free' public education guaranteed by Article 45 of the Constitution.

Certainly all rights, even the most basic rights, have their limits, including legal limits; consider the hackneyed example of freedom of speech and yelling 'Fire!' in a crowded theatre. Yet possession of a basic right such as freedom of speech is not conditioned on accepting some parallel duty. For example, while we may require a slanderer to provide restitution to his victim, he continues to have and be able to exercise a right to freedom of speech; the right (as a human or constitutional right) is independent of merit or the discharge of civic responsibilities.

The contingent rights granted by the state to Soviet citizens may be rights, but they are not human rights, or even the political implementation of human rights as legal or constitutional rights; they are held and enjoyed by numerous men and women in the Soviet Union, but they are not held as the rights of man. Marx himself, in a very early article, made the essential conceptual point quite clear in discussing freedom of the press: 'the *lack of rights* of the press is beyond all doubt once its *existence* is made dependent on its *frame of mind*' (1975:I, 316). Such 'rights' are contingent grants made by the state, not the inalienable entitlements of all persons or even all citizens.

Certainly there are theoretical alternatives to human rights-based regimes other than Soviet-style 'totalitarianism'. When we examine the existing governments of the world, however, the only prominent practical alternative (other than occasional Third World efforts at syncretic regimes, which we will discuss in the following section) seems to be authoritarianism of some sort. I would argue that the explanation for this lack is already clear from the discussion of Marx above, namely, the persistence of the state. The modern state presents us with a stark choice: either control it (through human rights or some demonstrably superior, or at least adequate, practice) or be controlled. Whatever their shortcomings, human rights-based regimes clearly make the right choice and, I would suggest, represent an appealing and relatively practical solution to the pressing problem of controlling the state.

Human Rights and the Third World

One common theme in many discussions of Third World conceptions of 'human rights' is the individualism of the 'Western' conception, i.e. the individualism of human rights as that concept has been discussed here. For example, Asmarom Legesse writes that in the West

> there is a perpetual, and in our view obsessive concern with the dignity of the individual, his worth, personal autonomy and property. (1980:124)
>
> If Africans were the sole authors of the Universal Declaration of Human Rights, they might have ranked the rights of communities above those of individuals. (1980:128)

Writing from an Islamic perspective, Ahmad Yamani likewise argues that the West 'is so overzealous in its defense of the individual's freedom, rights and dignity, that it overlooks the acts of some individuals in exercising such rights in a way that jeopardizes the community' (1968:15). Such claims usually lead to rather vague pleas for syncretic conceptions that combine the best of both approaches.

For example, Legesse argues that 'any system of ideas that claims to be universal must contain critical elements in its fabric that are avowedly of African, Latin American or Asian derivation' (1980:123). In practice this would mean the inclusion of group or peoples' rights along with individual human rights. However, the issues at stake in such a move demand a substantive, rather than a geographical, argument.

Human rights, as we have been discussing them, are held primarily by individuals[5] and they are exercised and claimed primarily in relation to society, usually in the person of the state. Peoples' rights, though, are held by society (again, usually in the form of the state) and directed against the individual (or other states) in their operation. If social rights and duties are both extensive and take priority over individual rights (as for example seems to be the case in the USSR), human rights are, as a practical political matter, likely to become merely formal.

In such circumstances, the right that one 'has' would be largely useless, not a trump at all, for in virtually all cases where one would want to claim it, the claim would be rather easily overridden. In other words, human rights would be effectively excluded from social and political action. In fact, as a practical matter one would be able to 'enjoy' the right only at the discretion of the state — but the state would not violate, or even infringe, the right in denying that enjoyment. This is much more like being granted a benefit than having a right.

It would appear, then, that human rights and peoples' rights can be combined only with great risk to the essential character of human rights; 'restoring the balance' between the individual and society in this fashion thus comes dangerously close to destroying human rights. In any case, 'having' such a 'human right' would be little like 'having a human right' as we have been using that phrase.

Furthermore, rather than demonstrate that particular rights are subject to such individualistic abuses and that the proposed remedy is preferable, all things considered, critics of the individualism of human rights tend instead simply to point out the undesirable side effects of certain human rights, without subjecting the proposed alternatives to similar scrutiny. The costs of abolishing (some) human rights may — or may not — be justified. A society that regularly balanced human rights against the rights of society may — or may not — be preferable to one based on the natural, inalienable rights of man. The issue, however, requires substantive arguments, not simply a recounting of now familiar cultural variations in political practices. While this is not the place to assess the relative merits of the claims of human rights and the rights of society, I do want to suggest that Third World writers seem to base their proposals on a wistful, largely anachronistic social vision.

The social model they seem to have in mind is the small community of extended family groupings so characteristic of (Western and non-Western) 'traditional' societies; in particular, a relatively decentralised, non-bureaucratic, communitarian society seems to be the envisioned ideal (compare Howard 1982). In such a society the individual lacks many, if not most, of the rights that are so highly valued in the liberal democratic state. However, he has a secure and significant place in his society and a wide range of intense personal and social relationships that provide major material and non-material support. He also has available regularised social protections of many of the values and interests that in the West today are protected through individual human, constitutional and legal rights.

One might argue that introducing individual rights into such a community would diminish, or at least fail to improve, the prospects for achieving a dignified life worthy of a human being. In any case, the organisation of such a society is easily defended on moral grounds, is in many ways quite attractive, and can be said to protect basic human dignity, in a plausible sense of that term; anthropological evidence might even be taken to suggest that such a communitarian solution is 'natural' to most peoples. However, if we remove the pressures of necessity and the social support and protection provided to the individual by the traditional community, it would be difficult to justify the continued absence of individual human rights while still having a system that could be said to protect and give prominence to human dignity.

'Westernisation', 'modernisation', 'development' and 'underdevelopment' — the dominant social and economic forces of our era

— have in fact severed the individual from the small, supportive community; and economic, social and cultural intrusions into, and disruptions of, the traditional community have removed the support and protection that would 'justify' or 'compensate for' the absence of individual human rights. A relatively isolated individual now faces social, economic and political forces that far too often appear to be aggressive and oppressive. Society, which once protected human dignity and provided each person with an important place in the world, now appears, in the form of the modern state, the modern economy and the modern city, as an alien power that assaults one's dignity and that of one's family.

In such circumstances, human rights appear as the 'natural' response to changing conditions, a 'logical' and 'necessary' evolution of the means for realising human dignity; the individual *needs* the protection of individual rights, barring the implausible, and generally undesired, re-emergence of the traditional order. And given the power of modern institutions, as well as the demonstrated inclinations of the individuals and groups that control them, not just any type of individual rights will do, but only rights with the (moral) force and range of universal human rights. In Marxist terms, the bourgeois economic revolution brings with it the bourgeois political revolution and bourgeois rights; capitalism and industrialisation bring in their wake natural or human rights, which, in such circumstances, represent a major advance in the protection of human dignity.

From this perspective, then, the 'individualism' of human rights appears as a response to objective conditions. Human rights are not the cause of the fragmentation of the traditional community, but an alternative mechanism to protect human dignity (defined in somewhat different terms) once such communities have been destroyed. Therefore, to deplore the individualism of human rights, in the absence of an alternative solution to the very real problems of protecting individual human dignity, is at best utopian or shortsighted.

This defence of human rights is admittedly only functional, and is based on a somewhat limited historical experience. None the less, it does suggest that the familiar argument that human rights are 'irrelevant' outside wealthy Western liberal democratic regimes is misguided. For example, Adamantia Pollis and Peter Schwab argue that 'it is evident that in most states of the world, human rights as defined by the West are rejected or, more accurately, are meaningless' and they refer to the Western concept as 'inapplicable', '[of] limited validity' and 'irrelevant' (Pollis and Schwab 1980:13, 8, 9). These are strong claims. For the most part, they are not justified.

Human rights are likely to be foreign to the average person in most developing countries, who might even have the greatest difficulty comprehending what is meant by 'human rights'. However, this is no more evidence that human rights are meaningless than similar difficulties in comprehension are evidence that '*dharma*' or '*tao*' are meaningless in Sioux Falls, or that 'quark' and 'gel electrophoresis' are meaningless just about everywhere. 'Inapplicable' or 'irrelevant' seem closer to what Pollis and Schwab have in mind, but even these terms have at least three important possible interpretations: that human rights objectively *have* no applicability; that their applicability is not *recognised*; or that the applicability of human rights is (or would be) *rejected*.

Determining the 'objective' relevance or irrelevance of human rights would be a most difficult matter. It is clear, however, that a simple demonstration that most people in a country have been, and continue to be, unaware of the concept, or have adopted alternative mechanisms for realising human dignity, will not establish that human rights are (objectively) irrelevant. Although a head count might be part of such a determination — and even that is not obvious — it certainly would not be definitive. A positive, substantive, probably even empirical, argument would be necessary to establish (objective) inapplicability.

The two subjective senses of 'irrelevant' raise problems of a different sort. For example, we are forced to ask what weight we ought to give to such subjective preferences and decisions as well as who is to speak for the society, and how. Such questions present us with at least partially competing intuitions. We must recognise the validity of claims of traditional values and institutions, as well as the rights of modern nations and states to choose their own destiny. At the same time, though, we feel a need to keep these choices constrained within acceptable bounds and reject an 'anything goes' attitude.

Certainly Louis XVI found the revolutionary rights of man to be 'inappropriate' — and today's historians seem to be not altogether certain that the majority of his subjects, especially outside of Paris, did not agree with him. More recently, 'Emperor' Bokassa and Idi Amin found human rights concerns, as traditionally understood, to be irrelevant, while Pol Pot and his successors alike determined human rights to be inappropriate to the needs and interests of

Cambodia. While there is widespread agreement that these men were and are 'wrong', elucidating the bases for such a conclusion, and then applying the resulting principles to less extreme cases, is quite difficult.

We might begin by suggesting that extreme cases such as Amin or Bokassa can be criticised on the basis of the concept of human dignity alone; the practices of such regimes evidence not alternative conceptions of human dignity but the denial of the very concept. For example, killing schoolchildren for protesting against school rules simply is incompatible with any and all plausible conceptions of human dignity. While claims of human rights would substantially increase the force of our condemnations of these regimes, we can both forcefully and appropriately condemn such practices on the basis of the concept of human dignity alone.

Problems arise, though, when we are faced instead with competing conceptions of human dignity. In these more common cases, Pollis and Schwab advocate extreme toleration for variations, coupled with an attempt to resolve differences at the international level through compromise or a lowest common denominator solution (1980:1, 14–17). But lowest common denominator and compromise approaches seem to assume (1) that the claim of human rights advocates and theorists that human rights are universal rights is false; and (2) that the human rights approach is not a 'better' one and therefore does not deserve to be more widely, let alone universally, applied. Such assumptions are not obvious, let alone obviously justifiable.

If we are to try to assess whether human rights is a 'better' way to approach human dignity and organise a polity, we need to ask 'Better than what?' This is a question of means, not ends. Human rights are not entirely ends in themselves; among other things, as we have seen, they are means to realise human dignity. To the extent that they have instrumental value, the merits of human rights can, at least in principle, be assessed largely empirically. I would suggest that for most of the goals of developing countries, *as defined by these countries themselves*, human rights are as effective as or more effective than either traditional approaches or modern non-human-rights strategies.

For example, if one's concern is with the realisation of human dignity, one could argue that the conditions created by modern-isation render the individual too vulnerable to social and economic indignities in the absence of human rights. If the concern is with development and social justice, a strong case might be made that the recognition and protection of human rights will increase participation, and therefore popular support and productivity; open up lines of communication between the people and government, resulting in greater efficiency and important checks against corruption and mismanagement; spur the provision of basic services through the recognition of economic and social rights; provide dispossessed groups with an important mechanism for demanding redress; and so forth (see Goodin 1979; Howard 1983; Donnelly 1984b). If one is concerned with stability, an argument might be advanced that a regime which violates or does not recognise basic human rights engenders destabilising opposition, especially where the government is weak and does not have at its disposal substantial, effective modern mechanisms of political control.

The case against the other assumption of those advocating compromise or a lowest common denominator strategy — namely, that human rights are in fact not universal rights — would have to be largely normative rather than empirical. The issue here boils down to whether there *are* human rights, since non-universal 'human rights' simply would not be human rights as they have heretofore been understood. The compromise strategy thus implies abandoning the idea of human rights not only without presenting arguments, but without even acknowledging the abandonment.

If we take seriously the notion of human rights, we must recognise them as both a historical product and universally valid; as human rights, they cannot be treated as merely historical products. In fact, the idea of human rights would seem to demand of us a concern for their universal realisation, even though we know that the concept was first formulated and institutionalised in a particular civilisation at a particular time. Such a demand is a difficult one, to be sure, but it is one that seems unavoidable if we are not to renounce human rights in the name of avoiding cultural neo-colonialism. Furthermore, it is not much more difficult than taking seriously any major moral claim, which we know arises out of values that are genetically contingent but which by their very nature must be taken to apply universally.

However, even if we grant, for the sake of argument, that human rights are not universal, the primary result will be to increase the importance of the questions of relevance and instrumental value considered briefly above. Simply establishing that human rights are not universal would not show that an alternative or competing approach to human dignity is necessarily defensible, let alone preferable. Rather, we would be left with several competing approaches which, unless we accept the crudest sort of value relativism, not only can, but must, be evaluated comparatively.

The differences between the human rights approach and such syncretic, communitarian approaches to human dignity certainly are large. However, they do not, in themselves, entail the necessity of a *laissez-faire* approach to the intellectual and political issues at stake. Neither do they establish the substantive merits of any particular syncretic strategy, let alone the inferiority of a universal human rights approach.

If the alternative approaches to political organisation and the realisation of human dignity we have been discussing are accepted as legitimate conceptions of human rights, the practice of human rights is likely to suffer. Not only would it become easier for a repressive regime to cloak itself in the mantle of human rights while actually violating them, thereby turning 'human rights' into an instrument of oppression rather than liberation, but in those countries with established human rights practices the theoretical underpinnings of the concept are likely to be eroded, thereby weakening the practice.

There is nothing in the concept of human rights that assures that it won't, let alone shouldn't, change or evolve; in fact, the constructivist theory is explicitly evolutionary. Strong arguments might even be made that it would be desirable to alter, reduce or minimise the place of human rights in political doctrine or practice. In light of all that has been said above, however, I think it is fair to insist that the more serious problem today is a shortage, rather than a surplus, of human rights.

Notes

1. Actually, the word Locke uses is 'power'. But 'power' for Locke means not just force or the ability to achieve something, but authority or right in the sense of 'having a right'. For example, in paragraph 1 he announces his intention to inquire into the true 'Original of Political Power', meaning the right to govern, as is particularly clear in paragraph 2 and as he makes explicit in paragraph 3: '*Political Power* then I take to be a *Right* of making Laws. . .'. Paragraph 4 likewise discusses 'Political Power', which by the end of the paragraph is being referred to as the 'Right to Dominion and Sovereignty'. Compare also paragraphs 7–9, 11, 24, 58, 82, 87, 199, 243.

Such a usage, now largely outdated, probably arises from the continued strong influence of Latin. (Some of Locke's own early writings are in Latin.) 'Power' translates the Latin *potestas*, which combines the senses of right or authority and capability or force in just such a fashion. This usage also rests on the continued vitality of the distinction between power (in this combined sense) and force, a distinction that has been lost in many realms of contemporary discourse.

2. This right is a right of society, for Locke, not a right of individuals (so long as society remains intact) (1967: paras 168, 211, 212, 243). This may, or may not, have some significance in a broader discussion of individualism and liberalism.

3. Mr Ivanov, Soviet Representative to the Economic and Social Council's Working Group on the Implementation of the International Covenant on Economic, Social and Cultural Rights, UN document number E/1980/WG.1/SR.14.

4. Compare recent diplomatic statements by the representatives of Romania, Ecuador and Iraq in UN documents number E/1980/WG.1/SR.4 and E/1980/WG.1/SR.7. For a recent expression of such a view by a liberal Western philosopher see Flew 1979:134. This seemingly more moderate view is no less misguided in making the possession of rights contingent on the discharge of logically entailed duties. For example, my property rights would not be forfeited by my trespassing on the property of others, and my constitutional right to due process or equal protection would in no significant way be affected should I regularly engage in illegal racial or sexual discrimination.

5. The exceptions usually represent a clear and rather explicit redefinition of the concept along the lines approved of in Legesse's argument. This is particularly evident in the case of the right to self-determination, which is included in the *Covenants* but not the *Universal Declaration*, and in the emerging 'third generation' of human rights, such as the rights to peace and development. See, e.g., UN documents number E/CN.4/1334 and HR/GENEVA/1980/BP.1–4, Alston 1980, and Marks 1981.

6 POSTSCRIPT: THE PROBLEM OF LISTS

While the questions of the nature and source of human rights have been fairly extensively addressed here, the third theoretical level, that of lists, has been scrupulously avoided.

If the constructivist theory adumbrated in Chapter 3 is sound, specification of a list of human rights will require the elaboration and defence of a philosophical theory of human nature. I hardly need emphasise the difficulty of such a task. Then the basic aspects of human nature that demand political protection through human rights would have to be 'translated' into particular rights. Since a single right might contribute to the realisation of several essential attributes or potentials, while several rights might contribute to the realisation of a single aspect of the identified human nature, the problems of 'translation' seem nearly as daunting as the substantive problems of elaborating the theory of human nature in the first place. Not surprisingly, I have concentrated on more manageable problems.

The work that I have done on the nature and source of human rights, however, can be seen as a necessary preliminary step towards a comprehensive and fully developed theory. And, for all its short-comings, it does seem to illuminate a number of important issues. It also begins to fill a serious gap in the literature.

For largely historical and practical reasons, the question of lists of human rights has been much more widely discussed than the logically prior questions of their nature and source. After World War II the subject of human rights was primarily the preserve of international lawyers and those working in or on international organisations, where major efforts were being devoted to the elaboration of international human rights standards, i.e. among those whose professional perspective emphasised the question of lists, and in arenas where lists were of immediate and intense concern. The immense political and technical problems of drafting, adopting and trying to implement international human rights declarations and treaties certainly would explain the reluctance to raise philosophical questions about the nature and source of human rights, questions that probably would only have generated irreconcilable conflicts.

When Jimmy Carter discovered human rights and tried to launch a new American human rights policy, lists again raised the only theoretical questions that seem to have been seriously considered; the underlying issues of the nature and source of human rights were largely glossed over in implicit and often unconscious decisions.

In addition, in both of these contexts the theoretical discussion was further reduced to the problem of the relationship between civil and political rights (such as the rights to life, security of the person and due process) and economic, social and cultural rights (such as the rights to work, social security and health care). Given that the status of economic and social rights was one of the great political issues in the Cold War-dominated UN human rights debates in the fifties and sixties, this focus is hardly surprising. But as neither side could ground its views in adequately developed conceptions of human nature and the nature of human rights, the debate remained essentially ideological. In particular, those who have argued that only civil and political rights are human *rights*, as opposed to social goals or other non-rights demands of justice, have done so without any sound conceptual foundation.

Consider, for example, Maurice Cranston's classic contemporary defence of the priority of civil and political rights. Cranston claims that while traditional civil and political rights to life, liberty and property are 'universal, paramount, categorical moral rights' (1964:40; 1973:25–50), economic and social rights are neither universal, practical, nor of paramount importance (1964:36–8; 1973:66–7). Therefore, economic and social 'rights' actually 'belong to a different logical category' (1964:54); they are not truly human rights.

As Cranston notes, many economic and social rights refer directly to a particular class of people, not to all human beings; for example, the right to periodic holidays with pay refers only to employees (1973:67). But many civil and political rights also fail such a test of 'universality'. For example, the rights to trial by a jury of one's peers and the presumption of innocence refer only to those accused of a crime, while the right to vote refers only to citizens who have attained a certain age and completed any necessary formalities of registration. Cranston's claim that the duties correlative to economic and social rights are not universal, while those correlative to civil and political rights are, is similarly false; for example, jury trial and equal protection impose duties primarily on the state.

In any society, especially complex modern societies, individuals participate in a variety of social institutions and assume a variety of roles, many of which have rights attached to them. Some of these roles may be considered basic and essential to the maintenance of one's dignity, so that anyone is a potential player of such a role, and when occupying that role is entitled to treatment of a certain type. This type of selection of basic roles or 'offices' underlies role-specific human rights. Since the class of potential 'office holders' is universal, and since most people can be expected to occupy such an office in the course of their lives, the rights in question are universal in a somewhat loose, but none the less significant, sense.

Traditional lists of civil and political rights single out the role of citizen for such protection, but there is no logical reason why other roles, such as worker or parent, cannot be similarly selected — and such selection yields important economic and social rights. Thus Cranston's argument must rest on a moral argument about the roles appropriately protected by human rights, an argument that itself must rest on a theory of human nature. He does not, however, provide such a theory or argument. In other words, Cranston's argument of universality, which he presents as a logical argument against economic and social rights, is at best a disguised and unsupported substantive moral argument.

The notorious right to paid holidays does seem far less important than, say, the right to life. However, even this right is hardly trivial or absurd. The full text of Article 7(d) of the *International Covenant on Economic, Social and Cultural Rights* reads 'rest, leisure and reasonable limitation of working hours and periodic holidays with pay, as well as remuneration for public holidays.' Rest and leisure can very plausibly be seen as essential to basic human dignity and thus worthy of protection through human rights; the denial of rest is a standard tactic in brainwashing, and the severely debilitating effects of excessive or unrelieved labour are beyond dispute.

In any case, periodic holidays with pay is hardly a typical economic and social right. For example, the right to work is arguably as important as most basic civil and political rights; the psychological, physical and moral effects of prolonged enforced unemployment may be as severe as those associated with the denial of freedom of speech. A right to education may be as important as freedom of speech or religion, or at least essential to a fully meaningful right to free speech or religion; for example, the assault of communist regimes on religion places great emphasis on the restriction of religious education. Similarly, rights to food and health care can be seen as extensions of the right to life required to give that right its full practical significance. While such arguments for the importance of economic and social rights certainly are controversial, they are no more contentious than competing arguments for the exclusion of economic and social rights. Supposedly conceptual argument often proves to be simply unsupported substantive moral argument.

Much the same is true of Hugo Adam Bedau's 'argument from primary goods'. A primary good is 'anything whatever that "a rational man wants whatever else he wants" '. Any rational man would want, at minimum and in particular, the protections provided by personal rights against state violations of one's person. Therefore, Bedau argues, civil and political rights[1] have the special force of primary goods (and, by implication, other rights don't) (1979:38). But certainly minimal food, water, shelter and health care are primary goods as well.

The derivation of a list of human rights rests on a substantive theory of human nature. Cranston and Bedau confuse a particular conception with the logical structure of human rights. There are a variety of plausible philosophical anthropologies that yield economic and social rights; those of Marx and Maslow come immediately to mind. If economic and social rights are to be excluded, these underlying theories must be taken on directly and in substantive terms.

Cranston's argument of practicality is a bit more complex than his others. ' "Political rights" can be readily secured by legislation. The economic and social rights can rarely, if ever, be secured by legislation alone' (1964:37). 'There is nothing especially difficult about transforming political and civil rights into positive rights', whereas the realisation of many economic and social rights is 'utterly impossible' in most countries (1973:66–7). Since rights impose correlative duties, and ought implies can (i.e. one has no obligation to attempt what is impossible), Cranston holds that it is logically incoherent to hold that economic and social 'rights' are anything more than utopian aspirations or ideals (1964:41; 1973:68).

While this argument is at least genuinely conceptual, it fares no better. Both the 'ought' and the 'can' in the moral maxim 'ought implies can' are slippery notions. When they are properly specified, the maxim proves to be of little relevance to questions of lists of human rights.

The 'ought' refers only to obligations all things considered, not to prima facie obligations. It may make perfectly good sense to say that one ought, prima facie, to do something that, on a more complete consideration of the factual and moral circumstances, proves to be 'impossible'. Since the obligations imposed by rights, despite their power relative to most other considerations, are only prima facie obligations, the 'oughts' in question seem not to be covered by the maxim.

In any case, the 'can' in 'ought implies can' refers simply to physical possibility. The impediments to implementing many if not most economic and social rights, however, are political rather than physical. Even 'the right of everyone to an adequate standard of living for himself and his family, including adequate food, clothing and housing' (*International Covenant on Economic, Social and Cultural Rights*, Article II), is arguably within the contemporary limits of *physical* possibility. We 'cannot' guarantee all people minimum food, clothing and shelter today largely because of political resistance to relatively egalitarian income distributions and other structural economic and political changes. For example, world food production is more than adequate to end starvation, and even malnutrition, but available supplies are distributed — for political, not physical or technological, reasons — so that hunger and malnutrition afflict hundreds of millions of people. Even paid holidays are well within the purely physical constraints of all countries today. 'Ought implies can' thus is irrelevant to the status of economic and social rights.

This leaves Cranston with little more than an argument that civil and political rights are relatively easy to implement. Bedau also presents a similar 'argument from indifference to economic contingencies' (1979:36-7). As we shall see in a moment, such arguments are empirically dubious. The more interesting question, however, is why they are perceived to be of any conceptual relevance at all. Why is relative ease of implementation seen as a logical rather than a merely technical consideration?

If such arguments have any conceptual basis, they rest on a distinction between 'negative' rights, which require only forebearance if they are to be realised, and 'positive' rights, which require the provision of goods and services, often in considerable quantity, if they are to be implemented and enjoyed. Both Cranston and Bedau suggest that because of their essentially 'negative' character, traditional civil and political rights deserve priority over economic and social rights. Henry Shue, however, shows that the distinction between positive and negative rights (a) fails to correspond to the distinction between civil and political and economic and social rights, and (b) in any case is of no moral significance.

Even such a quintessential 'negative' right as a right not to be tortured, generally will have a major 'positive' component. Simple restraint on the part of the government and its functionaries is necessary, but often insufficient in itself; in many countries, major changes in law, administrative practice and personnel would be necessary to guarantee the right. Institutions, with 'positive' powers, are needed to investigate allegations of torture and prosecute accused torturers. As Shue puts it, 'any reductions in torture are much more likely to be matters of prevention rather than self-discipline, and therefore of powerful positive initiatives against torturers' (1979:70). In fact, much more than mere legislation is required for the effective implementation of most rights, regardless of their type, and in many circumstances it is quite difficult indeed to translate civil and political human rights into law.

Shue also presents a powerful example (1980:41–6) to show that even an archetypical 'positive' right, such as the right to subsistence, may in some cases be essentially 'negative'. A peasant, who traditionally produces a quarter of his village's marketable food surplus, switches to growing flowers with the aid of labour-saving machinery in response to a government programme to increase export earnings from cash crops. Many other similarly situated peasants also alter their production, leading to reductions in the supply of food and sharp increases in its price. This in turn reduces food consumption by most marginal families, and even leads to severe malnutrition among the children of the workers displaced by the new machinery. But these infringements of subsistence rights could have been prevented by simple ('negative') governmental self-restraint in agricultural and development policy.

A formal statement of what a right is a right *to* simply will not tell us whether it is 'negative' or 'positive'. Shue argues that virtually all human rights are both 'negative' *and* 'positive', entailing ('negative') duties to forebear and ('positive') duties to protect and to aid — although there may be no single duty-bearer who stands under all three types of obligations. This is especially evident when we consider the varying actions which, depending on circumstances, may be required to discharge the obligation of the duty-bearer or guarantee the enjoyment of the right by the right-holder.

Furthermore, whether a particular right, as held by a particular person, is positive or negative depends at least as much on circumstances as on the essential character of the right. Protection from torture will be largely 'negative' in Mexico or Costa Rica, but 'positive' in Chile or Argentina. Subsistence will be a largely 'negative' right in the wheat fields of western Kansas, somewhat more 'positive' in New York City, and very 'positive' indeed in Bangladesh. The positive-negative distinction is not characteristic of rights *per se*, but of *particular rights in real circumstances*. Therefore, the character of any single right may change with time and place.

However, even if some particular human right or class of rights were entirely 'negative', Shue argues that they would not, *ipso facto*, deserve priority. Here the key theoretical issue is the moral significance of the distinction between acts of omission and acts of commission. This distinction underlies arguments such as Bedau's 'argument from analogy to crime', i.e. the argument that civil and political rights deserve priority because their violation involves the direct infliction of injury, and thus is strictly analogous to committing a crime, whereas violations of other rights, especially economic and social rights, usually only involve failing to confer a benefit (1979:38, compare Cranston 1964:38). Shue argues, however, that there is no important moral difference.

A man is stranded on an out-of-the-way desert island with neither food nor water. A sailor from a passing ship comes ashore, but leaves the man to die (an act of omission). This is as serious a violation of his rights as strangling him (an act of commission). It is killing him, plain and simple — indirectly, through 'inaction', but just as surely; perhaps even more cruelly (Shue 1979:72–5).

The moral difference lies not in the essential character of the acts *per se* (omission or commission) but in contingent, empirical circumstances. Determinations of priorities among rights must be based on the moral importance of the rights, rather than the changing, and largely arbitrary, nature of the ordinary type of violation of that right. As Shue suggests, following Judith Lichtenberg, the initial plausibility of the distinction rests on the fact that acts of commission usually are more likely to cause harm to the right-holder, while obligations that require positive acts are likely to be more burdensome to the duty-bearer. Where the costs and the consequences are the same, as where a sailor leaves another to die, that plausibility disappears.

Other arguments for the priority of civil and political rights stand up to scrutiny even less well. Consider, for example, Bedau's 'argument from the functional interdependence among basic rights' (1979:37–8). Without personal rights, economic and social rights are of little value, reducing people to 'hostages of fortune and patronized victims of tyranny.' Therefore, compared to the other basic types of rights, personal rights have a functional priority. But a true *inter*dependence rules out priority for any one class of rights. Interdependence suggests a mutual reinforcement of rights, so that they are more valuable together, as a complete package, than a simple summation of individual rights would suggest; for example, having civil and political rights but not economic and social rights is not 'half a loaf' but substantially less.

Standard arguments for the categorical priority of economic and social rights are equally misguided. It is often argued that civil and political rights, without economic and social rights, are mere formalities; that in the absence of minimum economic and social prerequisites, civil and political rights cannot be effectively enjoyed by most people. While often true — for example, starving people are not likely to be actively concerned with the right to vote — even in extreme cases the argument may be questionable. For example, much if not most debilitating poverty today is a political, not a natural, product, which might be remedied by the effective exercise of civil and political rights.

It still may turn out that one set of rights or another deserves pride of place. Previous arguments for such priority, however, simply will not stand up to scrutiny, because the categorical distinctions between classes of rights on which they have been based cannot survive careful examination. The reason for this is that previous arguments have failed to ground lists of human rights in a theory of their nature and source; most have not even shown an awareness of the need to do so.

The most important contribution of this book, in my view, is to provide a starting point for further work, and an indication of how to proceed — and what to try to avoid. We must return explicitly to moral conceptions of the human person, for example, as in the recent work of Alan Gewirth (1978, 1982a). Despite its difficulties, this is the theoretical frontier that must be explored and mastered before a comprehensive theory of human rights is possible.

Note

1. Actually, Bedau defends the priority of a class of civil and political rights, the so-called rights of the person, which 'bar others from interfering with one's conduct, and thus . . . demark a certain sphere of privacy, liberty or autonomy' (1979:35). For our purposes, however, this distinction is not relevant.

BIBLIOGRAPHY

Aarsleff, Hans (1969) 'The State of Nature and the Nature of Man in Locke', in John W. Yolton (ed.), *John Locke: Problems and Perspectives*, London: Cambridge University Press

Adams, E. M. (1982) 'The Ground of Human Rights', *American Philosophical Quarterly*, 19:191–5

Alston, Philip (1979) 'Human Rights and Basic Needs: A Critical Assessment', *Revue des droits de l'homme*, 12:19–68

——(1980) 'Peace as a Human Right', *Bulletin of Peace Proposals*, 11:319–30

Amalrik, Andrei (1977) 'A Well-fed Slave is a Well-fed Slave', *New York Times*, 3 February 1977 reprinted in Robert Woito (ed.), *International Human Rights Kit*, Chicago: World Without War Council

Aquinas, Saint Thomas (1913) *The 'Summa Theologica' of St Thomas Aquinas*, London: R. & T. Washbourne Ltd, 1913–25

——(1949) *On Kingship: To the King of Cyprus*, Toronto: Pontifical Institute of Medieval Studies

——(1959) *Aquinas: Selected Political Writings* (A. P. D'Entreves ed.), Oxford: Basil Blackwell & Mott Ltd

——(1963) *Summa Theologica* (Thomas Gilby ed.), Cambridge: Blackfriars

Arnold, Christopher (1978) 'Analyses of Rights', in Eugene Kamenka and Alice Ehr-Soon Tay (eds), *Human Rights*, New York: St Martin's Press

Ashcraft, Richard (1969) 'Faith and Knowledge in Locke's Philosophy', in John Yolton (ed.), *John Locke: Problems and Perspectives*, London: Cambridge University Press

Austin, John (1954) *The Province of Jurisprudence Determined*, London: Weidenfeld & Nicolson

Barnhardt, J. E. (1969) 'Human Rights as Absolute Claims and Reasonable Expectations', *American Philosophical Quarterly*, 6:335–9

Bay, Christian (1968) 'Needs, Wants and Political Legitimacy', *Canadian Journal of Political Science*, 1:242–60

——(1977) 'Human Needs and Political Education', in Ross

Fitzgerald (ed.), *Human Needs and Politics*, Rushcutters Bay, NSW: Pergamon Press (Australia)

——(1980) 'Peace and Critical Knowledge as Human Rights', *Political Theory*, 8:293–318

——(1981) *Strategies of Political Emancipation*, Notre Dame: University of Notre Dame Press

——(1982) 'Self-respect as a Human Right: Thoughts on the Dialectics of Wants and Needs in the Struggle for Human Community', *Human Rights Quarterly*, 4:53–75

Becker, Lawrence C. (1979) 'Three Types of Rights', *Georgia Law Review*, 13:1197–220

Bedau, Hugo Adam (1979) 'Human Rights and Foreign Assistance Programs', in Peter G. Brown and Douglas MacLean (eds), *Human Rights and U.S. Foreign Policy*, Lexington, Massachusetts: Lexington Books

Beitz, Charles R. (1979) 'Human Rights and Social Justice', in Peter G. Brown and Douglas MacLean (eds), *Human Rights and U.S. Foreign Policy*, Lexington, Massachusetts: Lexington Books

——(1981a) 'Economic Rights and Distributive Justice in Developing Societies', *World Politics*, 33:321–46

——(1981b) 'Democracy in Developing Societies', in Peter G. Brown and Henry Shue (eds), *Boundaries: National Autonomy and Its Limits*, Totowa, New Jersey: Rowman & Littlefield

Bender, Frederic L. (1981) 'World Hunger, Human Rights, and the Right to Revolution', *Social Praxis*, 8:5–30

Benn, Stanley I. (1967) 'Rights', *The Encyclopedia of Philosophy*, New York: Macmillan

——(1978) 'Human Rights — For Whom and for What?', in Eugene Kamenka and Alice Ehr-Soon Tay (eds), *Human Rights*, New York: St Martin's Press

—— R. S. Peters (1965) *The Principles of Political Thought*, New York: The Free Press

Bentham, Jeremy (1834) *Deontology* (John Bowring ed.), 2 vols, Edinburgh: Wm Tait

——(1838) *Works* (John Bowring ed.), 11 vols, Edinburgh: Wm Tait, 1838–43

——(1928) *A Comment on the Commentaries* (Charles Warren Everett ed.), Oxford: Clarendon Press

——(1931) *The Theory of Legislation* (C. K. Ogden ed.), London: Kegan Paul, Trench, Trubner & Co. Ltd

——(1948) *A Fragment on Government* (Wilfred Harrison ed.), Oxford: Basil Blackwell

——(1952) *Jeremy Bentham's Economic Writings* (W. Stark ed.), 3 vols, London: Allen & Unwin, 1952-4

——(1970) *Of Laws in General* (H. L. A. Hart ed.), London: The Athlone Press

Bergesen, Helge Ole (1979) 'Human Rights — The Property of the Nation State or a Concern of the International Community?', *Cooperation and Conflict*, 14:239-54

Berkowitz, Leonard (1969) 'Social Motivation', in Gardner Lindzey and Elliot Aranson (eds), *Handbook of Social Psychology* (second edition), Reading, Massachusetts: Addison-Wesley

Blackstone, William (1971a) 'Human Rights and Human Dignity', *The Philosophy Forum*, 9:3-37

——(1971b) 'On "Basic Political Rights" ', *Southern Journal of Philosophy*, 9:85-9

Boothby, Sir Brooke (1791) *A Letter to the Right Honourable Edmund Burke*, London: J. Debrett

Boulton, James T. (1963) *The Language of Politics in the Age of Wilkes and Burke*, London: Routledge & Kegan Paul

Bourke, Vernon (1956) 'Two Approaches to Natural Law', *Natural Law Forum*, 1:92-6

Bradley, F. H. (1962) *Ethical Studies*, Oxford: Oxford University Press

Brandt, R. B. (1964) 'The Concepts of Obligation and Duty', *Mind*, 73:374-93

Braybrooke, David (1972) 'The Firm But Untidy Correlativity of Rights and Obligations', *Canadian Journal of Philosophy*, 1:351-63

Brown, Peter G. and Douglas MacLean (eds) (1979) *Human Rights and U.S. Foreign Policy*, Lexington, Massachusetts: Lexington Books

Burke, Edmund (1869) *The Works of the Right Honourable Edmund Burke*, Boston: Little, Brown & Co.

Burns, J. H. (1966) 'Bentham and the French Revolution', *Transactions of the Royal Historical Society* (fifth series), 16:95-114

Buultjens, Ralph (1980) 'Human Rights in Indian Political Culture,' in Kenneth W. Thompson (ed.), *The Moral Imperative of Human Rights: A World Survey*, Washington, DC: University Press of America

Cavoski, Kosta (1982) 'The Attainment of Human Rights in Socialism', *Praxis International*, 1:365–75

Chalidze, Valery (1974) *To Defend These Rights*, New York: Random House

Chkhidvadze, V. (1980) 'Constitution of True Human Rights and Freedoms', International Affairs (Moscow), October: 13–20

Claude, Richard P. (ed.) (1976) *Comparative Human Rights*, Baltimore: The Johns Hopkins University Press

Cogley, John (ed.) (1963) *Natural Law and Modern Society*, Cleveland and New York: The World Publishing Co.

Cohen, Morris R. (1933) *Law and the Social Order*, New York: Harcourt, Brace & Co.

Copleston, F. C. (1955) *Aquinas*, Harmondsworth, Middlesex: Penguin Books

Coulson, N. J. (1957) 'The State and the Individual in Islamic Law', *International and Comparative Law Quarterly*, 6:49–60

Cox, Richard H. (1960) *Locke on War and Peace*, Oxford: Clarendon Press

Cranston, Maurice (1964) *What are Human Rights?*, New York: Basic Books

——(1973) *What are Human Rights?*, London: The Bodley Head

Cummings, Robert Denoon (1969) *Human Nature and History: A Study in the Development of Liberal Political Thought*, Chicago: The University of Chicago Press

D'Entreves, Alexander Passerin (1939) *The Medieval Contribution to Political Thought*, Oxford: Oxford University Press

——(1970) *Natural Law: An Introduction to Legal Philosophy*, London: Hutchinson University Library

Davies, James C. (1963) *Human Nature in Politics: The Dynamics of Political Behavior*, New York: John Wiley & Sons, Inc.

Donagan, Alan (1969) 'The Scholastic Theory of Moral Law in the Modern World', in Anthony Kenny (ed.), *Aquinas: A Collection of Critical Essays*, Garden City, New York: Anchor Books

Donnelly, Jack (1980) 'Natural Law and Right in Aquinas' Political Thought', *Western Political Quarterly*, 3:520–35

——(1982a) 'How Are Rights and Duties Correlative?', *Journal of Value Inquiry*, 16:287–94

——(1982b) 'Human Rights as Natural Rights', *Human Rights Quarterly*, 4:391–405

——(1984a) 'The Right to Development: How Not to Link Human Rights and Development', in Claude E. Welch and Ronald I. Meltzer (eds), *Human Rights and Development in Africa: Domestic, Regional and International Dilemmas*, Albany: State University of New York Press

——(1984b) 'Human Rights and Development: Complementary or Competing Concerns?', *World Politics*, 36:255–83

Dudley, James (1982) 'Human Rights Practices in the Arab States: The Modern Impact of Shari'a Values', *Georgia Journal of International and Comparative Law*, 12:55–93

Dunn, John (1968) 'Justice and the Interpretation of Locke's Political Philosophy', *Political Studies*, 16:68–87

——(1969) *The Political Thought of John Locke*, Cambridge: Cambridge University Press

Dworkin, Ronald (1977) *Taking Rights Seriously*, Cambridge: Harvard University Press

——(1978) 'Liberalism', in Stuart Hampshire (ed.), *Public and Private Morality*, Cambridge: Cambridge University Press

Egorov, A. G. (1979) 'Socialism and the Individual—Rights and Freedoms', *Soviet Studies in Philosophy*, 18:3–51

Eide, Asbjorn (1978) *Human Rights in the World Society: Norms, Realities and the International System of Protection*, Oslo: Universitetsforlaget

Ellin, Joseph (1965) 'Comments and Criticism: Wasserstrom and Feinberg on Human Rights', *The Journal of Philosophy*, 62:101–2

Ewing, A. C. (1947) *The Individual, the State and World Government*, New York: Macmillan

Ezorsky, Gertrude (1974) ' "It's Mine" ', *Philosophy & Public Affairs*, 3:321–30

Falk, Richard (1981) *Human Rights and State Sovereignty*, New York: Holmes & Meier

Feinberg, Joel (1964) 'Wasserstrom on Human Rights', *The Journal of Philosophy*, 61:641–5

——(1970) *Doing and Deserving: Essays in the Theory of Responsibility*, Princeton: Princeton University Press

——(1973) *Social Philosophy*, Englewood Cliffs: Prentice-Hall

——(1980) *Rights, Justice and the Bounds of Liberty: Essays in*

Social Philosophy, Princeton: Princeton University Press

Fisk, Milton (1978) 'The Human-Nature Argument', *Social Praxis*, 5:343–61

Fitzgerald, Ross (1977) 'Abraham Maslow's Hierarchy of Needs — an Exposition and Evaluation', in Ross Fitzgerald (ed.), *Human Needs and Politics*, Rushcutters Bay, NSW: Pergamon Press

Flathman, Richard E. (1977) *The Practice of Rights*, Cambridge: Cambridge University Press

——(1980) 'Rights, Needs and Liberalism: A Comment on Bay', *Political Theory*, 8:319–30

——(1982) 'Rights, Utility and Civil Disobedience', in J. Roland Pennock and John W. Chapman (eds), *Ethics, Economics and the Law*, New York: New York University Press

Flew, Anthony (1979) 'What is a Right?', *Georgia Law Review*, 13:1117–41

Foot, Philippa (1972) 'Morality as a System of Hypothetical Imperatives', *The Philosophical Review*. 81:305–16

Frankel, Charles (1978) 'Human Rights and Foreign Policy', *Headline Series*, 241 (October)

Fried, Charles (1978) *Right and Wrong*, Cambridge: Harvard University Press

Fuller, Lon L. (1958) 'Positivism and Fidelity to Law—A Reply to Professor Hart', *Harvard Law Review*, 71:630–72

——(1969) *The Morality of Law*, New Haven: Yale University Press

Galtung, Johan (nd) *Human Needs as the Focus of the Social Sciences*, Oslo: University of Oslo, Chair in Conflict Resolution

——and Anders Hekge Wirak (1977) 'Human Needs and Human Rights—a Theoretical Approach', *Bulletin of Peace Proposals*, 8:251–8

Gaus, Gerald F. (1981) 'The Convergence of Rights and Utility: The Case of Rawls and Mill', *Ethics*, 92:57–72

Gewirth, Alan (1978) *Reason and Morality*, Chicago: University of Chicago Press

——(1982a) *Human Rights: Essays of Justification and Applications*, Chicago: University of Chicago Press

——(1982b) 'Why Agents Must Claim Rights: a Reply', *The Journal of Philosophy*, 79:403–10

Gilson, Etienne (1956) *The Christian Philosophy of St Thomas Aquinas*, New York: Random House

Gluckman, Max (1964) 'Natural Justice in Africa', *Natural Law Forum*, 9:1–24

Goldstein, Kurt (1940) *Human Nature in the Light of Psychopathology*, Cambridge: Harvard University Press

——(1959) 'Health as a Value', in Abraham H. Maslow (ed.), *New Knowledge in Human Values*, New York: Harper & Brothers

Goldwin, Robert A. (1976) 'Locke's State of Nature in Political Society', *Western Political Quarterly*, 29:126–35

Goodin, Robert E. (1979) 'The Development-Rights Trade-off: Some Unwarranted Economic and Political Assumptions', *Universal Human Rights*, 1:31–42

——(1981) 'The Political Theories of Choice and Dignity', *American Philosophical Review*, 18:91–100

Grady, Robert C. (1976) 'Obligation, Consent and Locke's Right to Revolution: Who *Is* to Judge?', *Canadian Journal of Political Science*, 9:277–92

Green, Reginald Herbold (1981) 'Basic Human Rights/Needs: Some Problems of Categorical Translation and Unification', *Review of the International Commission of Jurists*, 27

Greenawalt, Kent (1982) 'Utilitarian Justifications for Observance of Legal Rights', in J. Roland Pennock and John W. Chapman (eds), *Ethics, Economics and the Law*, New York: New York University Press

Grisez, Germain G. (1965) 'The First Principle of Practical Reason', *Natural Law Forum*, 10:168–96

Haas, Ernst B. (1978) *Global Evangelism Rides Again*, Berkeley: Institute of International Studies

Haines, Charles Grove (1930) *The Revival of Natural Law Concepts*, Cambridge: Harvard University Press

Hakim, Khalifa Abdul (1955) *Fundamental Human Rights*, Lahore: Institute of Islamic Culture

Harakas, Stanley S. (1982) 'Human Rights: An Eastern Orthodox Perspective', *Journal of Ecumenical Studies*, 19:13–24

Hare, R. M. (1961)*The Language of Morals*, London: Oxford University Press

——(1982) 'Utility and Rights: Comments on David Lyons's Essay', in J. Roland Pennock and John W. Chapman (eds), *Ethics, Economics and the Law*, New York: New York University Press

Harman, Gilbert (1980) 'Moral Relativism as a Foundation for

Natural Rights', *Journal of Libertarian Studies*, 4:367–71

Hart, H. L. A. (1955) 'Are There Any Natural Rights?', *Philosophical Review*, 64:175–91

——(1958) 'Positivism and the Separation of Law and Morals', *Harvard Law Review*, 71:593–629

——(1961) *The Concept of Law*, Oxford: Oxford University Press

——(1972) 'Bentham on Legal Powers', *The Yale Law Journal*, 81:799–822

——(1973) 'Bentham on Legal Rights', in A. W. B. Simpson (ed.), *Oxford Essays in Jurisprudence (Second Series)*, Oxford: Clarendon Press

——(1977) 'Between Utility and Rights', in Alan Ryan (ed.), *The Idea of Freedom*, Oxford: Oxford University Press

Hassan, Riffat (1982) 'On Human Rights and the Qur'anic Perspective', *Journal of Ecumenical Studies*, 91:51–65

Hayek, F. A. (1976) *Law, Legislation and Liberty, Volume 2: The Mirage of Social Justice*, Chicago: The University of Chicago Press

Held, Virginia (1976) 'John Locke on Robert Nozick', *Social Research*, 43:169–95

Henkin, Louis (1978) *The Rights of Man Today*, Boulder, Colorado: Westview Press

Henle, Mary (ed.) (1961) *Documents in Gestalt Psychology*, Berkeley: University of California Press

Hersch, Jeanne (1970) 'Is The Declaration of Human Rights a Western Concept?', in Howard E. Kiefer and Milton K. Munitz (eds), *Ethics and Social Justice*, Albany: State University of New York Press

Hirscowitz, Marina (1966) 'The Marxist Approach', *International Social Science Journal*, 17:11–21

Hobbes, Thomas (1971) *Leviathan* (C. B. Macpherson ed.), Baltimore: Penguin Books

Hobhouse, L. T. (1922) *The Elements of Social Justice*, New York: Henry Holt & Co.

——(1925) *Morals in Evolution: A Study in Comparative Ethics*, New York: Henry Holt & Co.

Hocking, William Ernest (1926) *Present Status of the Philosophy of Law and of Rights*, New Haven: Yale University Press

Hohfeld, Wesley Newcomb (1923) *Fundamental Legal Conceptions*, New Haven: Yale University Press

Holmes, Oliver Wendell (1920) *Collected Legal Papers*, New York: Harcourt Brace & Co.

Hook, Sidney (1970) 'Reflections on Human Rights', in Howard E. Kiefer and Milton K. Munitz (eds), *Ethics and Social Justice*, Albany: State University of New York Press

Howard, Rhoda (1982) 'Is There an African Conception of Human Rights?', Working Paper No. A:8, Development Studies Programme, University of Toronto

——(1983) 'The "Full-Belly" Thesis', *Human Rights Quarterly*, 5:467–90

Hudson, Stephen D. (1979) 'A Note on Feinberg's Analysis of Legal Rights in Terms of the Activity of Claiming', *Journal of Value Inquiry*, 13:155–6

Husami, Ziyad (1980) 'Marx on Distributive Justice', in Marshall Cohen, Thomas Nagel and Thomas Scanlon (eds), *Marx, Justice, and History*, Princeton: Princeton University Press

Inada, Kenneth K. (1982) 'The Buddhist Perspective on Human Rights', *Journal of Ecumenical Studies*, 19:66–76

International Commission of Jurists (1982) *The Right to Development: Its Scope, Content and Implementation*, mimeo, January

International Labour Office (1976) *Employment, Growth and Basic Needs: A One-World Problem*, Geneva: International Labour Office

Ishaque, Khalid M. (1974) 'Human Rights in Islamic Law', *The Review of the International Commission of Jurists*, 12:30–9

Kamenka, Eugene and Alice Ehr-Soon Tay (eds) (1978) *Human Rights*, New York: St Martin's Press

Keenan, Edward L. (1980) 'Human Rights in Soviet Political Culture', in Kenneth W. Thompson (ed.), *The Moral Imperatives of Human Rights: A World Survey*, Washington, DC: University Press of America

Kelsen, Hans (1957) *What is Justice?*, Berkeley: University of California Press

Ketchum, Sara Ann and Christine Pierce (1981) 'Rights and Responsibilities', *Journal of Medical Philosophy*, 6:271–9

Khadduri, Majid (1946) 'Human Rights in Islam', *The Annals*, 243:77–81

Kleinig, Joel (1978) 'Human Rights, Legal Rights and Social Change', in Eugene Kamenka and Alice Ehr-Soon Tay (eds),

Human Rights, New York: St Martin's Press

Knutson, Jeanne N. (1972) *The Human Basis of the Polity: A Psychological Study of Political Men*, Chicago: Aldine, Atherton

Kohler, Wolfgang (1966) *The Place of Value in a World of Facts*, New York: Liveright Publishing Corporation

Kommers, Donald P. and Gilburt D. Loescher (eds) (1979) *Human Rights and American Foreign Policy*, Notre Dame: University of Notre Dame Press

Konvitz, Milton R. (ed.) (1972) *Judaism and Human Rights,* New York: W. W. Norton & Co.

Kumar, Satish (1981) 'Human Rights and Economic Development: The Indian Tradition', *Human Rights Quarterly* 3:47–55

Lachance, Louis (1965) *L'Humanisme politique de Saint Thomas D'Aquin: individu et état*, Paris: Editions Sirey

Lamont, W. D. (1950) 'Rights', *Aristotelian Society, Proceedings, Supplementary Volume*, 24

Landy, Frank J. and Don A. Trumbo (1976) *Psychology of Work Behavior*, Homewood, Illinois: The Dorsey Press

Lauterpacht, Hans (1950) *International Law and Human Rights*, New York: F. A. Praeger

Leclerq, Jacques (1957) 'Suggestions for Clarifying Natural Law', *Natural Law Forum*, 2:64–87

Legesse, Asmarom (1980) 'Human Rights in African Political Culture', in Kenneth W. Thompson (ed.), *The Moral Imperatives of Human Rights: A World Survey*, Washington, DC: University Press of America

Leng, Shao-Chuan (1980) 'Human Rights in Chinese Political Culture', in Kenneth W. Thompson (ed.), *The Moral Imperatives of Human Rights: A World Survey*, Washington, DC: University Press of America

Lo, Chung-Shu (1949) 'Human Rights in the Chinese Tradition', in *Human Rights: Comments and Interpretations*, a Symposium edited by UNESCO, London: Allan Wingate

Locke, John (1954) *Essays on the Law of Nature* (W. von Leyden ed.), Oxford: Clarendon Press

——(1967) *Two Treatises of Government* (Peter Laslett ed.), Cambridge: Cambridge University Press

——(1968) *The Educational Writings of John Locke* (James L. Axtell ed.), Cambridge: Cambridge University Press

——(1975) *An Essay Concerning Human Understanding* (Peter Nidditch ed.), Oxford: Clarendon Press

Lukes, Steven (1973) *Individualism*, New York: Harper & Row

——(1982a) 'Marxism, Morality and Justice', in G. H. R. Parkinson (ed.), *Marx and Marxisms*, Cambridge: Cambridge University Press

——(1982b) 'Can a Marxist Believe in Human Rights?', *Praxis International*, 1:334–45

Lyons, David (1969) 'Rights, Claimants and Beneficiaries', *American Philosophical Quarterly*, 6:173–85

——(1970) 'The Correlativity of Rights and Duties', *Nous*, 4:45–55

——(1973) *In the Interest of the Governed*, Oxford: Oxford University Press

——(1982) 'Utility and Rights', in J. Roland Pennock and John W. Chapman (eds), *Ethics, Economics and the Law*, New York: New York University Press

MacCormick, D. N. (1978) 'Dworkin as Pre-Benthamite', *The Philosophical Review*, 87:585–607

Macfarlane, L. J. (1982) 'Marxist Theory and Human Rights', *Government and Opposition*, 17:414–28

Machan, Tibor R. (1978) 'Against Nonlibertarian Natural Rights', *Journal of Libertarian Studies*, 2:233–8

——(1982) 'A Reconsideration of Natural Rights Theory', *American Philosophical Quarterly*, 19:61–72

Mackintosh, James (1927) *Vindicae Gallicae*, Philadelphia: William Young

Macpherson, C. B. (1963) *The Political Theory of Possessive Individualism*, Oxford: Oxford University Press

——(1977) 'Needs and Wants: An Ontological or Historical Problem?', in Ross Fitzgerald (ed.), *Human Needs and Politics*, Rushcutters Bay, NSW: Pergamon Press

Malik, Maqbul Ilahi (1981) 'The Concept of Human Rights in Islamic Jurisprudence', *Human Rights Quarterly* 3:56–67

Manglapus, Raul (1978) 'Human Rights Are Not a Western Discovery', *Worldview*, 4(October):4–6

Maritain, Jacques (1947) *The Rights of Man and Natural Law*, New York: C. Scribner's Sons

——(1951) *Man and the State*, Chicago: University of Chicago Press

Markovic, Mihailo (1982) 'Philosophical Foundations of Human .

Rights', *Praxis International*, 1:386–400

Marks, Stephen P. (1981) 'Emerging Human Rights: A New Generation for the 1980s?', *Rutgers Law Review*, 33:435–52

Marshall, Geoffrey (1973) 'Rights, Options and Entitlements', in A. W. B. Simpson (ed.), *Oxford Essays in Jurisprudence (Second Series)*, Oxford: Clarendon Press

Martin, Rex (1980) 'Human Rights and Civil Rights', *Philosophical Studies*, 37:391–403

——(1982) 'The Development of Feinberg's Conception of Rights', *Journal of Value Inquiry*, 16:29–45

Marx, Karl (1967) *Capital*, New York: International Publishers

——and Frederick Engels (1968) *Selected Works*, New York: International Publishers.

——(1975) *Collected Works*, New York: International Publishers, 1975–

Maslow, Abraham (1955) 'Deficiency Motivation and Growth Motivation', in Marshall R. Jones (ed.), *Nebraska Symposium on Motivation: 1955*, Lincoln: University of Nebraska Press

——(1959) 'Psychological Data and Value Theory', in Abraham H. Maslow (ed.). *New Knowledge in Human Values*, New York: Harper & Brothers

——(1968) *Toward a Psychology of Being*, Princeton: D. Van Nostrand Co.

——(1970) *Motivation and Personality*, New York: Harper & Row

——(1971) *The Farther Reaches of Human Nature*, New York: The Viking Press

Mathes, Eugene W. (1981) 'Maslow's Hierarchy of Needs as a Guide for Living', *Journal of Humanistic Psychology*, 21:69–72

——and Linda L. Edwards (1978) 'An Empirical Test of Maslow's Theory of Motivation', *Journal of Humanistic Psychology*, 18:75–7

Mawdudi, Abul A'la (1976) *Human Rights in Islam*, Leicester: The Islamic Foundation

Mayo, Bernard (1967) 'What Are Human Rights?', in D. D. Raphael (ed.), *Political Theory and the Rights of Man*, Bloomington: Indiana University Press

McCloskey, H. J. (1965) 'Rights', *The Philosophical Quarterly*, 15:115–27

——(1976) 'Human Needs, Rights and Political Values', *American*

Philosophical Quarterly, 13:1–11

McHale, John and Magda Cordell McHale (1979) 'Meeting Basic Human Needs', *The Annals*, 442:13–27

McKeon, Richard (1970) 'Philosophy and History in the Development of Human Rights', in Howard E. Keifer and Milton K. Munitz (eds), *Ethics and Social Justice*, Albany: State University of New York Press

Meddin, Jay (1976) 'Human Nature and the Dialectics of Immanent Sociocultural Change', *Social Forces*, 55:382–93

Melden, A. I. (1977) *Rights and Persons*, Berkeley: University of California Press

Messner, Johannes (1965) *Social Ethics: Natural Law in the Western World*, St Louis: B. Herder Book Co.

Miller, Richard W. (1981) 'Rights and Reality', *The Philosophical Review*, 90:383–407

Mitra, Kana (1982) 'Human Rights in Hinduism', *Journal of Ecumenical Studies*, 19:77–84

Morris, Arval (1981) 'A Differential Theory of Human Rights', in J. Roland Pennock and John W. Chapman (eds), *Human Rights*, New York: New York University Press

Morris, Herbert (1981) 'The Status of Rights', *Ethics*, 92:40–56

Moskowitz, Moses (1974) *International Concern with Human Rights*, Dobbs Ferry, NY: Oceana Publications Inc.

——(1979) 'Implementing Human Rights: Present Status and Future Prospects', in B. G. Ramcharan (ed.), *Human Rights: Thirty Years after the Universal Declaration*, The Hague: Martinus Nijhoff

Mukurjee, R. (1965) *The Social Structure of Value*, New Delhi: n.p.

Mulgan, R. G. (1968) 'The Theory of Human Rights', in K. J. Keith (ed.), *Essays on Human Rights*, Wellington: Sweet & Maxwell (NZ) Ltd

Nadvi, Syed Muzaffar-ud-Din (1966) *Human Rights and Obligations (in the Light of the Qur'an and Hadith)*, Dacca: S. M. Zahirullah Nadvi

Nagel, Ernest (1959) 'Fact, Value and Human Purpose', *Natural Law Forum*, 4:26–43

Nagel, Thomas (1959) 'Hobbes' Concept of Obligation', *Philosophical Review*, 68:68–83

Narveson, Jan (1967) *Morality and Utility*, Baltimore: The Johns Hopkins University Press

Newberg, Paula R. (ed.) (1980) *The Politics of Human Rights*, New York: New York University Press

Nielsen, Kai (1959) 'An Examination of the Thomistic Theory of Natural Moral Law', *Natural Law Forum*, 4:44–71

Oakeshott, Michael (1962) *Rationalism in Politics and Other Essays*, New York: Basic Books

Ogden, C. K. (1929) 'Bentham's Philosophy of "As-If" ', *Psyche* (London), 9:4–14

Olafson, Frederick A. (1966) 'Thomas Hobbes and the Modern Theory of Natural Law', *Journal of the History of Philosophy*, 4:15–30

Olivercrona, Karl (1974) 'Locke's Theory of Appropriation', *Philosophical Quarterly*, 24:220–34

Oppenheim, Felix E. (1968) *Moral Principles in Political Philosophy*, New York: Random House

Pagels, Elaine (1979a) 'The Roots and Origins of Human Rights', in Alice H. Henkin (ed.), *Human Dignity: The Internationalization of Human Rights*, New York: Aspen Institute for Humanistic Studies and Dobbs Ferry: Oceana Publications

——(1979b) 'Human Rights: Legitimizing a Recent Concept', *The Annals*, 442:57–62

Paine, Thomas (1945) *The Collected Writings of Thomas Paine*, (Philip S. Foner ed.), New York: The Citadel Press

Palumbo, Michael (1982) *Human Rights: Meaning and History*, Malabar, Florida: Robert E. Krieger Publishing Co.

Panikkar, R. (1982) 'Is the Notion of Human Rights a Western Concept?', *Diogenes*, 120 (Winter), 75–102

Parent, W. A. (1980) 'Judith Thomson and the Logic of Rights', *Philosophical Studies*, 37:405–18

Parkin, Charles (1956) *The Moral Basis of Burke's Political Thought*, Cambridge: Cambridge University Press

Pennock ,J. Roland and John W. Chapman (eds.) (1982) *Human Rights*, New York: New York University Press

Perelman, Ch. (1982) 'The Safeguarding and Foundation of Human Rights', *Law and Philosophy*, 1:119–29

Perry, Thomas D. (1977) 'Contested Concepts and Hard Cases', *Ethics*, 88:20–35

Piscatori, James P. (1980) 'Human Rights in Islamic Political Culture', in Kenneth W. Thompson (ed.), *The Moral Imperatives of Human Rights: A World Survey*, Washington, DC: University Press of America

Pitkin, Hanna Fenichel (1967) *The Concept of Representation*, Berkeley: University of California Press

——(1972) *Wittgenstein and Justice*, Berkeley: University of California Press

Plamenatz, John (1949) *The English Utilitarians*, Oxford: Basil Blackwell

Polish, Daniel F. (1982) 'Judaism and Human Rights', *Journal of Ecumenical Studies*, 19:40–50

Pollis, Adamantia and Peter Schwab (eds) (1980) *Human Rights: Cultural and Ideological Perspectives*, New York: Praeger Publishers

Pound, Roscoe (1926) *Law and Morals* (second edition), Chapel Hill: The University of North Carolina Press

——(1960) 'Natural Natural Law and Positive Natural Law', *Natural Law Forum*, 5:70–82

Priestley, Joseph (1791) *Letters to the Right Honourable Edmund Burke Occasioned by His Reflections on the Revolution in France, &c.*, Birmingham: Thomas Pearson (sold by J. Johnson, London)

Rai, Lal-dhoj Desoa (1981) 'Human Rights and Development in Ancient Nepal', *Human Rights Quarterly*, 3:37–46

Rawls, John (1955) 'Two Concepts of Rules', *Philosophical Review*, 64:3–32

——(1974) 'The Independence of Moral Theory', *Proceedings and Addresses of the American Philosophical Society*, 48:5–22

——(1980) 'Kantian Constructivism in Moral Theory', *The Journal of Philosophy* 78:515–72

Raz, Joseph (1979) *The Authority of Law: Essays on Law and Morality*, New York: Oxford University Press.

Renshon, Stanley (1974) *Psychological Needs and Political Behavior*, New York: The Free Press

——(1977) 'Human Needs and Political Analysis: an Examination of a Framework', in Ross Fitzgerald (ed.), *Human Needs and Politics*, Rushcutters Bay, NSW: Pergamon Press

Richards, David A. J. (1979) 'Human Rights and the Moral Foundations of the Substantive Criminal Law', *Georgia Law Review*, 13:1395–446

——(1981) 'Rights and Autonomy', *Ethics*, 92:3–20

Riley, Patrick (1974) 'On Finding an Equilibrium Between Consent and Natural Law in Locke's Political Philosophy', *Political Studies*, 22:432–52

—— (1976) 'Locke on Voluntary Agreement and Political Power', *Western Political Quarterly*, 29:136–45

Ritchie, David G. (1895) *Natural Rights*, New York: Macmillan & Co.

Rommen, Heinrich (1949) *The Natural Law*, St Louis: B. Herder Book Co.

Rosan, Laurence J. (1971) 'Human Rights and Human Dignity in the Philosophy of Absolute Idealism', *The Philosophy Forum*, 9:99–105

Rosen, Frederick (1977) 'Basic Needs and Justice', *Mind*, 86:88–94

Rosenbaum, Alan S. (ed.) (1980) *The Philosophy of Human Rights: International Perspectives*, Westport, Connecticut: Greenwood Press

Roshwald, Mordecai (1959) 'The Concept of Human Rights', *Philosophy and Phenomenological Research*, 19:344–79

Ross, Alf (1959) *On Law and Justice*, Berkeley: University of California Press

Ross, W. D. (1930) *The Right and the Good*, Oxford: Clarendon Press

Rous, George (1791a) *A Letter to the Right Honourable Edmund Burke in Reply to His Appeal from the New to the Old Whigs*, London: J. Debrett

—— (1791b) *Thoughts on Government occassioned by Mr Burke's Reflections, &c. . . .* London: J. Debrett

Said, Abdul Aziz (1977) 'Pursuing Human Dignity', *Society* 15:34–8

—— (1979) 'Precept and Practice of Human Rights in Islam', *Universal Human Rights*, 1:63–80

—— (1980) 'Human Rights in Islamic Perspectives', in Adamantia Pollis and Peter Schwab (eds), *Human Rights: Cultural and Ideological Perspectives*, New York: Praeger Publishers

Sapontzis, S. F. (1978) 'The Value of Human Rights', *Journal of Value Inquiry*, 12:210–24

Sawczuk, Konstantyn (1979) 'Soviet Juridical Interpretation of International Documents on Human Rights', *Survey*, 24:86–91

Scanlon, Thomas (1975) 'Thomson on Privacy', *Philosophy & Public Affairs*, 4:315–22

Schacter, Oscar (1976) 'The Evolving International Law of Development', *Columbia Journal of Transnational Law*, 15:1–16

Scheffer, Samuel (1979) 'Moral Independence and the Original Position', *Philosophical Studies*, 35:397–403

Schoeman, Ferdinand (1977) 'The Harm Principle and a Theory of Natural Rights', *The Journal of Value Inquiry*, 11:235–43

Searle, John R. (1969) *Speech Acts*, Cambridge: Cambridge University Press

Seliger, Martin (1963) 'Locke's Theory of Revolutionary Action', *Western Political Quarterly*, 16:548–68.

Sen, Amartya (1982) 'Rights and Agency', *Philosophy & Public Affairs*, 11:3–39

Shue, Henry (1979) 'Rights in the Light of Duties', in Peter G. Brown and Douglas MacLean (eds), *Human Rights and U.S. Foreign Policy*, Lexington, Massachusetts: Lexington Books

——(1980) *Basic Rights: Subsistence, Affluence and U.S. Foreign Policy*, Princeton: Princeton University Press

Sidgwick, Henry (1897) *The Elements of Politics*, London: Macmillan & Co.

Silving, Helen (1955) 'The Twilight Zone of Positive and Natural Law', *California Law Review*, 43:477–513

——(1958) 'Positive Natural Law', *Natural Law Forum*, 3:24–43

Simpson, Evan (1982) 'The Priority of Needs over Wants', *Social Theory and Practice*, 8:95–112

Singer, Marcus (1964) 'Lamont on Rights and Duties', *Philosophy and Phenomenological Research*, 26:112–16

——(1972) 'The Basis of Rights and Duties', *Philosophical Studies*, 23:48–57

Singer, Peter (1972) 'Famine, Affluence and Morality', *Philosophy & Public Affairs*, 1:229–43

Sohn, Louis B. and Thomas Buergenthal (1973) *Basic Documents on International Protection of Human Rights*, Indianapolis: Bobbs-Merrill

Sommerville, John (1949) 'Comparison of Soviet and Western Democratic Principles, with Special Reference to Human Rights', in UNESCO, *Human Rights: Comments and Interpretations*, London: Allen Wingate

Spiegelberg, Herbert (1971) 'Human Dignity: A Challenge to Contemporary Philosophy', *The Philosophy Forum*, 9:39–64

Srzednicki, J. (1971) 'Rights and Rules', *The Philosophical Quarterly*, 21:315–23

Stanlis, Peter J. (1965) *Edmund Burke and the Natural Law*, Ann Arbor: The University of Michigan Press

Sterba, James P. (1979) 'The Moral Presuppositions of Contractual Rights', *Ethics*, 89:298–305

——(1981) 'Human Rights: A Social Contract Perspective', in *Proceedings of the American Catholic Philosophical Association*

Stone, Julius (1946) *The Province and Function of Law*, Sydney: Associated General Publications

——(1965) *Human Law and Human Justice*, Stanford: Stanford University Press

Strauss, Leo (1953) *Natural Right and History*, Chicago: University of Chicago Press

Streeten, Paul (1979) 'Basic Needs: Premises and Promises', *Journal of Policy Modeling*, 1:136–46

Tabandeh, Sultanhussein (1970) *A Muslim Commentary on the Universal Declaration of Human Rights*, London: F. T. Goulding & Co.

Taurek, John S. (1977) 'Should the Numbers Count?', *Philosophy & Public Affairs*, 6:293–316

Thakur, Ramesh (1982) 'Liberalism, Democracy, and Development: Philosophical Dilemmas in Third World Politics', *Political Studies*, 30:333–49

Thompson, E. P. (1966) *The Making of the English Working Class*, New York: Vintage Books

Thompson, Kenneth W. (ed.) (1980) *The Moral Imperatives of Human Rights: A World Survey*, Washington, DC: University Press of America

Thomson, Judith Jarvis (1971) 'A Defense of Abortion', *Philosophy & Public Affairs*, 1:47–66

——(1973) 'Rights and Deaths', *Philosophy & Public Affairs*, 2:146–59

——(1975) 'The Right to Privacy', *Philosophy & Public Affairs*, 4:295–314

——(1976) *Self-Defense and Rights*, The Lindley Lecture, University of Kansas

——(1977) 'Some Ruminations on Rights', *Arizona Law Review*, 19:45–60

Tuck, Richard (1979) *Natural Rights Theories*, Cambridge: Cambridge University Press

Van de Veer, Donald (1980) 'Are Human Rights Inalienable?',

Philosophical Studies, 37:165–76

Vasak, Karel (1977) 'Human Rights', *UNESCO Courier*, November: 29

——(ed.) (1978) *Les dimensions internationales des droits de l'homme*, Paris: UNESCO

Veatch, Henry (1969) 'The Defense of Natural Law in the Context of Contemporary Analytic Philosophy', *American Journal of Jurisprudence*, 14:54–68

——(1978) 'Natural Law: Dead or Alive?', *Literature of Liberty*, 1:7–31

Vlastos, Gregory (1962) 'Justice and Equality', in Richard B. Brandt (ed.), *Social Justice*, Englewood Cliffs: Prentice-Hall

Wahba, Mahmoud A. and Lawrence G. Bridwell (1976) 'Maslow Reconsidered: A Review of Research on the Need Hierarchy Theory', *Organizational Behavior and Human Performance*, 15: 212–40

Wai, Dunstan M. (1980) 'Human Rights in Sub-Saharan Africa', in Adamantia Pollis and Peter Schwab (eds), *Human Rights: Cultural and Ideological Perspectives*, New York: Praeger Publishers

Walzer, Michael (1977) *Just and Unjust Wars: A Moral Argument with Historical Illustrations*, New York: Basic Books

Wasserstrom, Richard (1964) 'Rights, Human Rights and Racial Discrimination', *Journal of Philosophy*, 61:628–40

Watt, E. D. (1982) 'Human Needs, Human Wants, and Political Consequences', *Political Studies*, 30:533–43

Weil, Simone (1973) *Oppression and Liberty*, Amherst: University of Massachusetts Press

Weinstein, Michael A. (1971) 'Basic Political Rights', *Southern Journal of Philosophy*, 9:75–84

Weldon, T. D. (1953) *The Vocabulary of Politics*, Harmondsworth, Middlesex: Penguin Books

Wertheimer, Max (1961) 'Some Problems in the Theory of Ethics', in Mary Henle (ed.), *Documents in Gestalt Psychology*, Berkeley: University of California Press

Westermarck, Edward (1912) *The Origin and Development of the Moral Ideas*, London: Macmillan & Co.

Williams, Peter C. (1978) 'Losing Claims of Rights', *Journal of Value Inquiry*, 12:178–96

Wittgenstein, Ludwig (1958) *Philosophical Investigations*, New York: The Macmillan Co.

Wollstonecraft, Mary (1791) *Vindication of the Rights of Man*, London: J. Johnson
——(1795) *An Historical and Moral View of the Origins and Progress of the French Revolution; and the Effect it has produced in Europe*, London: J. Johnson
——(1967) *Vindication of the Rights of Woman*, New York: W. W. Norton & Co.
Yamani, Ahmad Zaki (1968) *Islamic Law and Contemporary Issues*, Jidda: The Saudi Publishing House
Yolton, John (1969) *John Locke: Problems and Perspectives*, London: Cambridge University Press

INDEX